DESIGNING RELATIONSHIPS
THE ART OF
COLLABORATION IN
ARCHITECTURE

In today's dynamic practice environment, collaboration skills are increasingly critical to the successful completion of building projects. Indeed, it is the careful nurturing of comradeship among complementary but distinctive egos that drives creativity underlying the hi-tech algorithms that help shape complex projects.

Designing Relationships focuses on the skill set necessary to facilitate effective collaboration among all stakeholders no matter what project delivery mode or technology is deployed. This book provides valuable guidance on how to design and construct buildings in a team context from inception to completion. It is the less tangible elements of collaboration that provide the magic that transforms the most challenging projects into great works of architecture, and it is these more nuanced and subtle skills that the book brings to the fore.

The emergence of integrated project delivery and building information modeling together with the complexity of projects and the speed with which they must be completed make an in-depth understanding of collaboration a current, critical issue in architectural practice.

Andrew Pressman, FAIA, an architect, Professor Emeritus at the University of New Mexico, and Lecturer at the University of Maryland, leads his own architectural firm in Washington, DC. He has written numerous critically acclaimed books and articles, and holds a Master's degree from the Harvard University Graduate School of Design.

DESIGNING RELATIONSHIPS

THE ART OF COLLABORATION IN ARCHITECTURE

ANDREW PRESSMAN

 Routledge
Taylor & Francis Group

LONDON AND NEW YORK

First published 2014
by Routledge
2 Park Square, Milton Park, Abingdon, Oxon OX14 4RN

and by Routledge
711 Third Avenue, New York, NY 10017

*Routledge is an imprint of the Taylor & Francis Group, an informa
business*

Every effort has been made to contact and acknowledge copyright
owners. The publishers would be grateful to hear from any copyright
holder who is not acknowledged here and will undertake to rectify any
errors or omissions in future printings or editions of the book.

The publisher and author disclaim any liability, in whole or in part,
arising from information contained in this publication. The reader is
urged to consult with an appropriate licensed professional prior to
taking any action or making any interpretation that is within the realm
of a licensed professional practice.

British Library Cataloguing in Publication Data
A catalogue record for this book is available from the British Library

Library of Congress Cataloging in Publication Data
Pressman, Andy.
Designing relationships : the art of collaboration in architecture /
Andrew Pressman.
pages cm
Includes bibliographical references and index.
1. Group work in architecture. I. Title.
NA1995.P74 2014
720.68--dc23
2013025045

ISBN: 978-0-415-50627-4 (hbk)
ISBN: 978-0-415-50628-1 (pbk)
ISBN: 978-1-315-85235-5 (ebk)

Typeset in Helvetica Neue LT Pro 9/13pt
by Fakenham Prepress Solutions, Fakenham, Norfolk NR21 8NN

Printed and bound in Great Britain by
TJ International Ltd, Padstow, Cornwall

Dedicated to Lisa, Daniel, and Samantha.
I cannot imagine being
part of a better collaborative team.

**Never underestimate the power
of a small dedicated group of people
to change the world.**

—ATTRIBUTED TO MARGARET MEAD[1]

**Losers assemble in little groups and
bitch about the coaches and the system
and other players in other little groups.
Winners assemble as a team.**

—BILL PARCELLS[2]

The team is a genius.

—WILLIAM CAUDILL[3]

NOTES

1. John Abele, "Bringing Minds Together," *Harvard Business Review*, vol. 89 no. 7/8, July–August 2011, p. 88.

2. Michael Lewis, "What Keeps Bill Parcells Awake at Night," *The New York Times Sports Magazine*, November 2006, p. 51.

3. William W. Caudill, *Architecture by Team*, New York: Van Nostrand Reinhold, 1971, p. 239.

CONTENTS

FOREWORD

Orchestrating *intangibles* such as human interaction and collaboration in support of a tangible outcome presents a significant challenge for the professional. *Designing Relationships* demonstrates how collaborative dynamics, communication, leadership, and other intangible processes can be cultivated, managed, and merged with technological tools to produce the synergistic emergence of a successful building.

In *Designing Relationships,* the author first presents rationale for interpreting collaboration based on time-tested operational principles, explaining how design can improve processes and systems within the architecture, engineering, and construction (AEC) industry. Subsequent chapters—in addition to examining varieties of "managed" approaches to collaboration and styles of leadership and teamwork—introduce recent technological tools now commonly used (building information modeling—BIM), and contractual structures commonly known but relatively limited in current use (integrated project delivery—IPD). I would add a third element—a strategic methodology originally associated with automotive manufacturing and more recently adapted to the AEC industry called Lean Construction.[1] Not surprisingly, BIM, IPD, and Lean are sophisticated and work best in high-functioning collaborative teams working on complex projects.[2]

When the BIM model is used by high-functioning teams, it can be an incredibly powerful tool. Not only does it have capacity to maintain large quantities of data in accessible graphic form, the protocols designed to develop the model rely on collaborative dialogue, positive decision-making, and clear communication. For BIM to support teams in this way, significant time must be invested in early planning for BIM's use, development of clear strategies for transition of model "ownership" between parties, and frequent adjustment and monitoring of procedures. Consistent effort must be made to ensure file management protocols are followed, information is reliable to specified levels of tolerance, and uses of the model are clear.

On the other hand, while these tools and processes can greatly reduce risk for a high-performing team, their use cannot salvage a complex project that suffers from poor collaboration. For example, BIM can exacerbate distrust and create impediments to communication. If communication is poor or lack of trust leads to defensive behavior, the BIM model can become a battleground. Ownership of information may come under dispute, leading to excessive tracking and reporting on every aspect of the model. BIM models contain a great deal of information, and in a situation where trust is lacking, addressing disputes over each data point could consume time rather than save it.

For low-risk projects—those using conventional processes, known systems, and a straightforward program—BIM, IPD, and Lean can result in lost time and increased tension. BIM may be more effective in its non-interactive mode, serving as three-dimensional documentation for the architect to generate two-dimensional views. In general, low-risk projects can use relatively simple communication tactics and basic strategies to achieve success.[3]

Just as using BIM does not assure smooth communication, the use of an IPD model does not ensure alignment and trust. Used together, BIM and IPD can be a very effective set of tools for a team to enable great communication, efficient collaboration that is both streamlined and innovative, and to cement a culture of trust and respect that leads to success. IPD is essentially the written contractual assurance that the team will "play well together" with minimal contractual barriers to collaboration. Lacking case law, the question remains—can subjectively defined behavior be regulated with IPD contracts?[4] While elements of IPD contracts such as shared risk and reward pools have produced documented savings and innovation, the "softer" language around mutual trust and respect have less tangibly measured effects and results. Whether in a contract or not, whether for high-functioning teams or low-risk projects, those soft skills as elaborated in *Designing Relationships* are necessary for a cohesive collaborative effort.

Even the simplest building project requires many interrelated actions to go well in order to achieve success. And in most success stories, collaboration plays a large role. Often considered a happy by-product of a good team, we are increasingly aware that it is the other way around—groundwork must be set forth to achieve good collaboration. *Designing Relationships* does a great service to the AEC industry by demystifying the techniques, mindsets, and strategies that together form the art of collaboration.

Renée Cheng, AIA, Professor
Head of the School of Architecture, College of Design
University of Minnesota

NOTES

1. Authoritatively documented by the Lean Construction Institute, http://leanconstruction.org.

2. For more specific information comparing the "degree of IPD" among different projects; see the author's report, http://aia.org/ipdcasestudies2011, done in collaboration with Katy Dale, Research Fellow at University of Minnesota and sponsored by AIA and AIA Minnesota.

3. This observation comes from preliminary results of a collaborative research project by the author and Katy Dale, Research Fellow at University of Minnesota, with the invaluable help of Gina Neff and Carrie Dossick from University of Washington.

4. Howard Ashcraft, Patrick O'Connor and other leading legal professionals in construction law have shared thoughts on this topic in numerous publications.

PREFACE

*D*esigning Relationships: The Art of Collaboration in Architecture* is intended to bring architects—and everyone involved in the architectural/engineering/construction industry—up to speed on how to get the most out of collaboration by (1), discussing collaboration basics applied to architectural practice, and interpreting and synthesizing state-of-the-art insights from business and management worlds as well as precedents from other disciplines. At a minimum, this should improve architects' relationships and effectiveness with their internal design teams and external consultants, clients, and other project stakeholders. And by (2), breaking new ground on effective collaborative design processes to assist in achieving design excellence and a competitive advantage. Therefore, this is more than a simple guidebook; it challenges the status quo—and the reader—to think critically about collaboration, and to change the design process from project inception to completion.

The book will elaborate on project-based collaborative processes for designing and constructing buildings, termed *managed collaboration*. With the power of a "managed" form of collaboration you may significantly enhance survival in today's economy, gain a competitive advantage, work more efficiently cross-culturally and globally, differentiate your practice more readily, solve complex problems, and more boldly engage projects of scale. *Designing Relationships* suggests how aspects of a managed style may be integrated with a more traditional approach to orchestrating a given team and project, in a manner that a given leader can embrace most comfortably. Truly effective collaboration of any style is a means for architects to reassert their leadership in the design of buildings.

Learning to collaborate effectively and reaping the resulting benefits could not be more timely. The emergence of integrated project delivery (IPD) and building information modeling (BIM) together with the complexity of projects and the speed with which they must be completed make an in-depth understanding of collaboration a current, critical issue in architectural practice.

Ideas are woven throughout *Designing Relationships* supporting the notion that collaboration must be taken seriously as a multidimensional process with rigorous

cipline in contrast to casual teamwork. For example, taking time to critically reflect
. the collaborative process may be essential to its successful outcome: Viewing
intrinsic tension, discord, or opposing viewpoints as constructive on the path to a
solution instead of seeing these as simply annoying can serve as a relevant, even
liberating insight. "Teamwork" has become ubiquitous, and is used as a buzzword
to connote anything from a very casual group encounter or one-time work session
to participating on a committee. Collaboration, on the other hand, requires a studied
commitment to a sequenced, multilevel process with discrete magnitude and
direction.

Designing Relationships is for leaders who want to grow their collaborative leadership
skills and elicit the best work from partners and collaborators. And it is for team
members who seek insights to better job performance and better project outcomes.

This book will address scales of collaboration from one-on-one design critiques,
to internal architectural design team charrettes, to brainstorming with the entire
spectrum of project stakeholders including architects, consulting engineers, cost
consultants, constructors, owners, and others in a project's community.

The process of inquiry and collaboration is a design problem itself for each project.
Design of the service delivery presents a great opportunity to apply our unique skill
set in developing the most effective process. Tailored appropriately, a collaborative
process can be applied across diverse project types, clients, and delivery systems.
In this way, a deliberate, calculated, even aggressive strategy can be designed
for a specific project. This is what will make both project delivery and the project
distinctive. As project leader, the architect can adjust the collaborative approach
to the required matrix of specialties, personalities, tasks, and circumstances—and
determining how and when collaboration occurs—to yield the best possible design.
Here is where the art of what I am identifying as "managed collaboration" is manifest.

During a challenging economic period in which a scarcity of work may leave key
staff with increased amounts of downtime, there is an opportunity to examine, hone,
and reflect on the art of multidisciplinary collaboration and teamwork. Acquired and
polished skill sets will update the firm's process patterns and ultimately confer an
advantage in the marketplace in terms of appealing to prospective clients. It cannot
be overstated that for firms to not only survive but also prosper, collaboration—
specifically tuned for architectural practice—must be an integral part of the project
delivery process.

There is no formula or easy algorithm for collaborating but the variables can be
described, analyzed, and then optimized to produce the best possible architecture.
Designing Relationships: The Art of Collaboration in Architecture attempts to set forth
a framework in which this may be accomplished.

Cooperation is a natural social characteristic in animal and primate realms.[1] However, among humans, there are variables that interfere with that tendency such as the deadly sins of politics, greed, money, power, and ambition. In addition, the traditional design–bid–build delivery process in contemporary architectural practice positions the architect and contractor as natural adversaries and has elevated liability concerns, potential for litigation, and risk management strategies to the extent that the natural predisposition for collaboration is in a down cycle. *Designing Relationships* revisits the benefits of working together while mitigating the negative consequences.

Charles Darwin[2] was prophetic when he said, "In the long history of humankind, those who learned to collaborate and improvise most effectively have prevailed." Learning to collaborate effectively under the spiritual and substantive guidance of a real leader—with the right attitude, compelling goals, talent, and commitment—will ensure that a firm evolves to provide great service, innovation, and design.

Andrew Pressman, FAIA
Washington, DC
June 2013

NOTES

1. Martin A. Nowak, "Why We Help," *Scientific American*, vol. 307 no. 1, July 2012, pp. 36–39.

2. Charles Darwin. www.charlesdarwinonline.com/#quotes (accessed February 12, 2013).

ACKNOWLEDGMENTS

I am truly grateful for the support, critical guidance, and professionalism of Francesca Ford, Commissioning Editor at Routledge, who enthusiastically advocated the idea for the book. I deeply appreciate the work of the design and production team at Routledge/Taylor & Francis including Emma Gadsden, Senior Editorial Assistant, Alanna Donaldson, Production Editor, and Liz Dawn, Copy-Editor.

The following individuals deserve special mention for keen editorial advice, guidance, or reviews of the proposal and manuscript: Catharine Lisa Kauffman (especially for the brilliant title), Charles Linn, Len Charney, Mark C. Childs, Peter Pressman, Cliff Moser, Randy Deutsch, and Robert Ivy.

Much appreciation is extended to Renée Cheng for writing the Foreword; and to the contributors of the "Snapshots" of Chapter 5—Mark Childs (again!), David Riz (and Chris Macneal and Carin Whitney for facilitating David's essay), Roger Schwabacher (and Brian Kelly for suggesting Roger), Andrew Deschenes (and Jeff Millett for referring me to Andy), and Stephen D. Dent.

Special thanks to Iris Slikerman, and Dennis Pelletier (of Yarmouth Printing and Graphics) for their graphic talent and assistance.

Portions of this work are based on previously published articles by the author, including:

"It's a Very Good Time to Develop Your Firm's Collaboration Skills," *Architectural Record*, vol. 197 no. 4, April 2009, pp. 47–48.

"Creating a Firm Culture that Supports Innovative Design," *Architectural Record*, vol. 196 no. 2, February 2008, pp. 65–66.

"Good Leadership Helps Practice, the Profession, and Society," *Architectural Record*, vol. 195 no. 9, September 2007, pp. 79–80.

"Integrated Practice in Perspective: A New Model for the Architectural Profession," *Architectural Record*, vol. 195 no. 5, May 2007, pp. 116–120.

Images are by Andrew Pressman unless otherwise noted.

No matter how you look at it, architecture—as manifest in a building—is a collaborative effort. It may not be a great collaborative effort but it is almost invariably the result of constructors, clients, consulting engineers, and the architect working together in some way. This collective effort ought to be acknowledged, supported, and celebrated in an effort to strive for and reinforce excellence in the work. Some architects who receive media accolades as stars and as sole authors of buildings are really not accurately portrayed. It takes a team to realize projects of scale or complexity. There may be a prominent and aggressive project leader, but it does indeed "take a village."

COLLABORATION DEFINED

Collaboration is a collective intellectual function that can be a force multiplier in an effort to reach an intended objective. In a general sense, collaboration represents a device for leveraging resources. Collaboration requires efficient

1

INTRODUCTION TO COLLABORATION

communication channels between all levels, dimensions, and distances for those striving toward an objective in synergistic fashion. Collaboration requires well-defined process, rigorous discipline, and critical reflection throughout time.

Creating a work of architecture is a collaborative effort. No doubt about it. As I have noted, it takes architects, engineers, clients, product manufacturers, cost estimators, and constructors to create a building. Someone has to assemble the collaborators, lead the effort and ensure that the overarching idea for the building is supported — and built upon — every step of the way, and that it is not compromised by the team effort. And the primary way for the team to remain focused, inspired, and effectively collaborating is to sustain a structure for the collaborative effort.

There is a spectrum of collaborative activities and styles. Collaboration can range from a casual comment in the midst of a phone conversation or as a result of a napkin sketch that triggers new ideas, or during a work session that includes well-choreographed brainstorming toward creation of various alternative solutions to vexing problems.

Critiquing each other's work is a form of simple collaboration. Everyone benefits from bouncing ideas off someone else, talking to just one other person can clarify a proposition or perhaps suggest an alternative path of investigation, or even modify a good idea to make it better — that's the most basic form of collaboration. Even if the other person says nothing, the simple act of talking out loud can spur the elaboration of an idea or, similarly, an individual's comments can elicit a new idea or approach from someone else.

John Cleese of Monty Python fame captured the essence of a collaborative process in the following vignette.

> *The really good idea is always traceable back quite a long way, often to a not very good idea which sparked off another idea that was only slightly better, which somebody else misunderstood in such a way that they then said something which was really rather interesting.* [1]

It is implicit in this funny account that knowledge is freely exchanged, can be misinterpreted, but somehow becomes synergistic. The serious and sometimes accidental business of generating a good idea is enjoyable for a skilled yet diverse team.

Another example of collaboration in action is a songwriting session with Adele, the British soul singer, and Paul Epworth, a songwriter and producer. This is a universal experience and could just as well be a brainstorming session in any number of disciplines. Mr. Epworth describes it as follows.

> *A good musical collaboration is like a Jackson Pollock of musical paint, where everyone's throwing ideas at a canvas and some of them stick and some of*

them don't, and the final picture you end up with is a combination. She'd come forth with an idea, and I'd say, "How about this," and it develops and hybridizes on its own into something.[2]

Incorporation of critical comments almost always translates to an opportunity to make the work even more potent. Change does not have to be viewed as compromise, rather it is something that can potentially make a project more responsive to a client requirement, an aesthetic priority, a technical issue, site circumstance, and so on.

Conversations and critiques can serve to question the status quo, the preconceptions and automatic design responses to what may appear to be typical problems. Conversations and critiques, then, can be considered a fundamental type of collaboration. A great example of this was the Works in Progress program of the Boston Society of Architects. An architect would present a project in process, and chapter members—and occasionally others from allied disciplines such as artists, landscape architects, or planners—would assemble to constructively critique the design work of one of their colleagues. This happened out of the office context and away from the pressures of a business environment. There is great benefit to this type of external, collaborative review. Fresh eyes, unimpeded by explicit or implicit agendas, can be focused on design quality and introduce new perspectives. The more exposure there is to diversity in points of view, the more possibilities become evident. Benefits also accrue to the reviewers. Experience in evaluating the work of others will improve collaborative and interpersonal skills, and will also contribute to more objective and effective self-criticism.

Attitude is important. Everyone on a team has an obligation to strive for the group's success. Roger Goldstein, FAIA,[3] Principal at Goody Clancy, believes that attitude has more to do with building rapport than anything else. He says, "Being respectful of peoples' contributions, even if you disagree or think some ideas are not worthwhile, helps on the trust dimension," and inevitably will reinforce the habit of vocal contribution.

Scott Simpson, FAIA,[4] Principal and Senior Director at the Cambridge, MA, office of KlingStubbins, elaborates on attitude:

Collaboration is an attitude more than a process. Participants assume that each member of the team has something valuable to offer, and that by using many brains synergistically rather than working in "silos," overall outcomes will be dramatically improved. In a collaborative effort, it is understood that different points of view add richness and depth to the project, but this means that ego must take a back seat.

I hasten to qualify Simpson's point; opposing viewpoints may also slow progress and create impasse. This is where a team leader must intervene and keep the effort moving ahead. There is a delicate balance between promoting discussion of conflicting ideas that may lead to innovation and knowing when to advance the work.

RATIONALE FOR COLLABORATING

The ability to work effectively in teams has become increasingly important because of the complexity of projects requiring expertise from a variety of specialties and demands from clients for better building performance. Collaboration is a meaningful response to the ongoing marketplace mandate for buildings that are faster to design and construct and at lower cost than those built in the past. And, perhaps most important, it could be argued that the final outcome—the design work—is actually better. Michael Schrage[5] takes it one step further: "Collaboration does not curtail the architect's overarching vision. Collaboration becomes a medium that makes the vision possible." There could be no better time for seizing the opportunity to establish and fine-tune the notion of team practice and collaboration.

The following list underscores the urgency and need for multidisciplinary collaboration in creating architectural designs.

▓ ***The requirement for environmentally sensitive and sustainable architecture.*** The conventional wisdom is that multidisciplinary collaboration must occur at project inception—and conception—if sustainable or environmentally sensitive outcomes are to be successful.

▓ ***Unstable and recessionary economic trends.*** Especially during these times, clients require the assurance of an optimal cost-effective and efficient process with reliable quality in outcomes.

▓ ***Innovations in technology.*** This includes integrated project delivery (IPD) and building information modeling (BIM). By definition, these models of practice, which are increasingly required by clients, are inherently collaborative. See Chapter 4 for a detailed discussion on this topic.

▓ ***Globalization of architecture.*** Culturally, environmentally, and economically sensitive design is at a premium. Collaboration provides a means to deliver appropriate architectural services internationally.

▓ ***Contractual and liability issues.*** These concerns have heretofore impeded the best possible collaborative environment for multidisciplinary participants, and are starting to be addressed by the American Institute of Architects (AIA) in the second iteration of contract documents, by sophisticated clients and firms who are advocating risk-sharing and risk-allocation provisions in alliancing contracts, by professional liability insurance carriers, and by the participants themselves.

- **Competitive advantage can be achieved through strategic collaborations.**
  The caveats, of course, are that everyone must embrace their respective roles
  and work together well.

The inefficiencies inherent in the process of design and construction are neces-
sitating a shift to greater multidisciplinary collaboration and information sharing
among project team members. In our current practice environment, as the list above
suggests, it is simply no longer sufficient to execute projects on time and within
budget while maintaining the status quo.

WHY HAVE ARCHITECTS BEEN INHERENTLY NONCOLLABORATIVE?

There are many forces that collectively and progressively have tended to make
architects work in isolation and that must be unlearned or overcome in order to be
successful at collaborating. Here are some examples of those forces; acknowledging
and recognizing them may help to actively surmount the problems.

- Architects learned the habit of designing only by themselves in architecture
  school. Many academic programs still implicitly celebrate a subculture in which
  graduates spend their careers working as heroic, solitary, isolated designers. This
  attitude has been represented and perpetuated by the Howard Roark character
  in Ayn Rand's *The Fountainhead,*[6] which remains a best-selling novel even today.
  Roark summarized the point: "No great work is ever done collectively, by a
  majority decision. Every creative job is achieved under the guidance of a single
  individual thought." But integrated project delivery—and all the reasons why
  collaboration is necessary in today's practice environment—is fueling a rethinking
  of that exclusive notion.

- In design–bid–build, the conventional form of procuring architectural and
  construction services, the architect and contractor are natural adversaries. The
  tension that exists between the parties is intended to be part of a system of
  checks and balances for the good of the project. The architect typically advocates
  for quality and delight—a better product—while the contractor's interest in the
  project is usually economic. This tension has, in the past, generally resulted in
  successful buildings. However, in the current practice context, there is a strong
  rationale for multidisciplinary collaboration (as described above). Therefore, the
  adversarial process must be replaced on many projects by a completely different
  mindset, with all stakeholders working together for the good of the project.

- The volume of litigation in the construction industry has contributed to defensive,
  noncollaborative, risk-averse behavior.

"Norman won't collaborate."

Figure 1.1   Notwithstanding this image of the heroic, solitary designer, cooperation is a
natural social characteristic in animal and primate realms. We must cultivate
this innate tendency to work successfully in multidisciplinary creative teams.
(Robert Weber / The New Yorker Collection / www.cartoonbank.com.)

■ The importance of establishing a professional reputation based on one's own
body of work—either in academia or the profession—is considered necessary
for career advancement in many cases. Faculty in schools of architecture do not
become tenured professors unless they can demonstrate national and international renown based on their own individual portfolio of scholarly and creative
work. As role models, that certainly has an influence on all of their students.
In terms of professional recognition, many architects covet design awards and
publications precisely because these honors celebrate individuals, not typically
teams. The attention that is associated with this publicity helps architects to
market their services and acquire commissions.

WHEN NOT TO COLLABORATE

Architecture requires a certain amount of collaboration with engineering consultants on all but the smallest-scale projects. However, the great caution, of course, in the realm of collaboration is that the work is indeed amenable to a team approach and that an individual could not better or more efficiently execute it. It must be recognized that some challenges (or parts of some challenges) are best met by one good performer—or well-seasoned professional. Moreover collaboration can consume lots of time and resources. Therefore, in the master plan of executing a project, *there will be an amalgamation of teamwork and individual work in some ideal proportions* as designated by the architect/leader.

GENERAL AXIOMS THAT SUPPORT TRADITIONAL COLLABORATIVE DYNAMICS

What follows are 11 statements promoting collaboration in architecture. They represent conventional wisdom, are occasionally counterintuitive, and may even be provocative.

1. *Do not automatically trust your fellow team members.* Develop rapport and respect instead. It is unrealistic to trust team members with whom you have had little contact. Trust is not a necessary prerequisite for effective collaboration; respect is. Professional judgment and expertise are very important in establishing common language, rapport, and respect. Having a beer, sharing a meal, giving a gift, or experiencing a good time does not define the notion of "trust." These events do not and should not engender trust. Trust is cultivated over many years through shared adversity as well as smooth sailing.

2. *Malignant narcissism is important for effective teamwork.* Do not check your ego at the door. Do not insist that others check their egos at the door. Confidence, and even a bit of arrogance are helpful to innovate and to transcend mediocrity. Sometimes those with great ideas are motivated to invoke a measure of theatrics to awaken a stagnant team. But, at the same time, others' valuable contributions or roles must be acknowledged. In any case, individuals must always be acknowledged for their contributions to the team effort and to advancing the project. There is nothing wrong with a healthy ego that is responsible for pushing the design envelope.

3. *Work independently to collaborate better.* Collaborators must take individual responsibility for their own area of expertise—or role on the project—as a prerequisite to creating a synergistic, collective work product above and beyond individual contributions. There is an "I" in collaboration. That's how much of the

work gets accomplished. Moreover, a colleague can be stoked up and inspired by another's clever work—or another's vacuous work, which leads to the next statement, below.

4. **Bad ideas are essential.** Bad ideas are great because they often trigger exceptional ideas from others. So the bad idea must be appreciated; that is, all ideas need to be considered, nurtured, then rejected, accepted, or built upon—not immediately crushed—as an integral part of the collaborative process. The secondary benefit of not automatically casting off the bad idea is to save face for the collaborator who proposed it, bolstering his or her ego, and enabling fruitful participation in the future.

5. **Teamwork can dilute powerful ideas.** This is especially true without strong leadership from the architect. Never underestimate the power of the majority to slow and even suffocate the creative individual or the iconoclast. The leader is charged with mitigating peer pressure or emergent norms that may reflect an apathy of the team.

6. **Effective teamwork is significant independent of technology and tools.** All too often technology is nothing more than distraction. Preoccupation with technical hardware and/or software inevitably narrows a designer's frame of reference, may result in blind spots or myopia, and may remove one from the real world of textures, subtleties, nuances, and constantly changing patterns.

7. **The best leadership is plastic, not necessarily transparent.** To lead well, design an approach to elicit the best work from each collaborator as a function of their personality, the task at hand, and the project circumstances. Leaders should tailor their interventions to specific collective and individual styles.

8. **Personality can be misleading in selecting an optimal collaborative team.** Time and again the more seductive personality is chosen over the more creative or effective professional. Do not select the more facilitative personalities, rather recruit individuals whose background and skills best complement the team and support the project at hand. Playing nice is important but overrated. Team chemistry can be an elusive but critical variable.

9. **Great design can be achieved as much by an individual as by a collaborative effort.** The cliché argument, "What is better: the auteur or the team?" is a meaningless academic exercise. It just depends on both the individuals involved and the project challenges. Approach and method should be adjusted to the context. The leader must be prepared to improvise.

10. **A great team could be characterized as one big unhappy dysfunctional family.** You don't have to like the other team members to have a great team and produce great results. Project and personal agendas—intrinsic

motivations—transcend this. Tension between team members can be seen as constructive—as the gasoline that fuels innovation and excellent work.

11. **Collaborate with your fiercest competition.** Add great strength, networks of consultants and clients, knowledge, and insight to a particular project. In other words, keep friends close, enemies closer.

TRADITIONAL COLLABORATIVE BASICS

Some clichés apply to collaborating in architecture. Here are a few axioms in which a traditional mode of collaborative performance can be cultivated and sustained.

- *Overarching noble theme and agenda that motivates every single team member.* Provide a vision—a set of shared aspirations—together with specific goals that everyone buys into. Take full advantage of the great intrinsic motivation and passion in architecture—evoke the collective goal that launches most prospective architects into the profession—to create excellent, beautiful designs, even magical places to live, work, and play. Another example of such an overarching vision is sustainability. It should not be too difficult to get everyone on board with that—in fact, that vision will help to attract the best talent to your firm. Focus on (1) the transcendent nature of architecture in general (i.e. the notion that you are providing a professional service, which is truly distinctive in society); firm mission; and professional and personal agendas—this is easy with architecture because it is part of every architect's DNA (it is the core of what architects are taught to do). And (2) the design idea for a specific project. Here is where individual agendas should intersect or align with the collective agenda of making great architecture. It cannot be underscored enough that intrinsic motivation is a key to a successful collaborative effort from all team members. Leaders should focus on this because it is even more important than social skills. In sum, creatively and cleverly framed design challenges, proffered at every phase of a project, are intrinsically motivating and lead to higher productivity and quality.

- *Seek diversity in team composition.* This applies to experiences, background, culture, worldview, and area of expertise. The more diverse—and the more potential for creative tension—the more likely there will be innovative ideas and solutions to challenging problems. In other words, celebrate differences to promote design excellence. Collaborators who know each other well want to work together but that can tend to produce mediocre results and narrow-minded group-think. One way the architect can prevent this from happening is by selecting new consultants with fresh perspectives for the design team.

- *Only collaborate strategically—not on every task.* Not all tasks are amenable to collaborative work. In fact, within a given project, the best outcomes result when the architect knows when to assign tasks to a team and when to assign tasks to an individual. In general, *individual* preparation prior to engaging in *collaborative* work can optimize productivity and outcomes.

■ ***Provide effective leadership.*** The leader must ensure that there are not too many good ideas on the table, and that compromise does not dilute a strong idea. The leader should present ideas to be elaborated upon almost like giving an "assist" in basketball so that another talented player can take the idea, build on it, and slam dunk it—or make it better. The leader must ensure that each collaborator feels that their individual contribution has been meaningful to the progress of the collective work so that they can legitimately claim investment in and ownership of the design. See discussion, "Leading collaborative projects," in Chapter 3.

■ ***Be mindful of the soft skills; learn them and practice them.*** With the promulgation of powerful new software tools such as BIM, understanding collaborative behavior is just as important as understanding the technology. Even though these psychological and communication skills are not as valuable as genuine expertise, they can greatly facilitate collaboration. See more on soft skills below.

■ ***Have fun to innovate and create.*** Derive satisfaction from and promote a sense of fun—and humor (while still taking the work seriously)—in interactions with others. If the interactions are fun, there is a greater likelihood of project success, that is, deeper understanding of stakeholder issues and a better environment to cultivate innovative ideas. The gratification of working on a successful collaborative effort is incomparable.

■ ***Promote innovation and risk taking to get the best design work.*** No idea should be deemed too precious to hold on to like grim death. Conversely, every idea should be taken seriously and thought of as a potential contribution to be built upon. Don't judge (at least don't make judgments too quickly). Treat new ideas with particular attention and sensitivity; do not let them be crushed. Acknowledge unsuccessful work as a valuable part of the collaborative process and as an opportunity to learn. The IDEO mantra, now a cliché, "Fail often to succeed sooner"[7] is particularly salient.

■ ***Take time to critically reflect on the collaborative process, both during the project and after.*** Analogous to the morbidity and mortality (M & M) conference in medicine, this is a means of retrospectively and critically analyzing every detail of a failure or bad outcome so as to heighten awareness of pitfalls and increase the probability of better outcomes in the future. What was successful, what didn't work, what would you do differently on the next project, what was good that you should build upon in the future? Become mindful of your own role in the process; evaluate your participation in the team effort—was it substantive, tangential, constructive, too much, too little? Were you an active listener? Did you acknowledge criticism or dismiss it?

- ▨ ***Every team and every project is different.*** Design the collaborative process accordingly; there is no formula. All team members must buy into the specific process of the project as defined by the architect.

- ▨ ***Assume responsibility.*** All design team members must take individual responsibility for their respective areas of expertise in the context of working for the good of the project.

A productive, collaborative work session requires talented people who are empowered to make decisions on behalf of their firms and who are unafraid to push disciplinary boundaries. Integrated concepts cannot evolve successfully without the participation of all relevant disciplines with the architect leading the way, eliciting ideas and comments.

Building rapport, goodwill, and respect among all the multidisciplinary players is also essential to the best collaborative sessions. How do you do that? "Transparency, openness, and a willingness to share information," states Jim Summers,[8] an Associate in the Boston office of Burt Hill, "will enable the change of focus from individual to project." Their team members will spend a significant amount of time together to understand a clear scope of responsibilities, design objectives, degree of risk, and bottom line; this "fleshing out" is part of the discovery process, resulting in a contract that supports a unique workflow. Summers is amazed at "the soft skills you need to work through that process and come to an agreement," *and this is even before the project itself starts.*

Some of the soft skills that can be sharpened to make you a better collaborator include establishing rapport and respect, active listening, speaking, writing, drawing, negotiating, and using humor—all toward enhancing truly reciprocal communication between all collaborators. Here is some elaboration on the benefits of employing those skills.

Rapport. If there is such a thing as the standard condition for engaging people, it is rapport. To have rapport with another, be yourself; you should neither affect some wooden formality you may believe is "professional" nor be excessively casual and familiar. In the case of collaborating with a client, the client's perception that he or she is being *cared for* will likely enhance participation, the quality of information offered, and wishes voiced.

Respect. Respect everyone else on the team; presumably they are on the team because they have a certain level of expertise. Respect the project and client. Try to resist the natural inclination to judge people. This is especially true for collaborators.

Rather, focus on the project and the design work to realize the great vision and to implement the concepts.

Active listening. Try to appreciate your collaborator's unique perspectives. Focusing on what a collaborator says—how they say it, and why they say it—sets the stage for interpreting ideas and incorporating them into the design. If an idea represents a genuine contribution, acknowledge and celebrate it, and the collaborator will be that much more invested in the project.

Speaking and writing. Architects can't advocate the value of architecture, much less their good ideas, if they can't communicate well to both nonarchitects and those in the profession. Avoid jargon and pseudo-academic gobbledygook. Instead, use a style that is "clean, straightforward, focused, vigorous, serious but not solemn, friendly but not flippant."[9]

Drawing. Architects have a huge advantage in working collaboratively because they can use the universal language of drawing as a means to create, communicate—and even play—with others. Drawing is effective in communicating ideas across cultures and diverse stakeholders. Fully exploit this skill that uniquely distinguishes architects in brainstorming sessions and one-on-one.

Negotiating. Architects can creatively apply negotiating strategies to numerous situations beyond contracts, such as collaborating on a design. For example, in the classic text, *Getting to Yes: Negotiating Agreement Without Giving In,*[10] the authors describe a method they term "principled negotiation." This method includes four basic tenets: separate people from the problem, focus on interests as opposed to positions, invent options for mutual gain, and insist on objective criteria. Further, they suggest recasting personal attacks as attacks on the problem itself.

Humor. Infusing conversations and meetings with humor might just be one of the most important strategies in successfully engaging collaborators—and in establishing rapport. Humor can also help to diffuse frank criticism or comments without having them appear as a personal attack.

There is consensus that there is nothing better than face-to-face sessions to foster collaboration and meaningful relationships. This is particularly true at the start of a project when even one such meeting will pave the way for a year of subsequent videoconferences. Socializing can also help a group to coalesce into a team. However, it must be stated that social ties can also lead to maladaptive relationships, disruption of a chain of command, serious distraction, and even disaster.

COMMON ELEMENTS IN COLLABORATIONS ACROSS DISCIPLINES

There are a number of common elements in successful collaborations across disciplines. The following describes some of them that are applicable to architecture. They are common sense and self-evident, but they are important reminders.

- Differences among team members are encouraged in order to solve challenging problems in innovative fashion. These include differences in background, experience, and, most importantly, ideas. Perhaps it is the creative tension (expressed in a collaborative context)—often between practical exigencies and ideals—that motivates innovation and keeps creativity tied to the solution of (sometimes) mundane but significant problems. Discussion of conflicting ideas should be promoted; conflicts between people should not be permitted.

- Reflect on and process the criticisms and dialogue of the collaborative sessions.

- Regarding team composition, assemble the best and brightest talents as the highest priority to yield the best ideas and results. The softer skills of working together are of lesser importance, albeit valuable.

- Collaborative skills—working constructively with others—are best developed through experiences, and actively reflecting on those experiences.

- Excellent preparation is as important as spontaneity during a collaborative session.

- Honestly share expertise, knowledge, ideas, and criticisms. In other words, promote genuinely reciprocal communication.

A COLLABORATIVE SCENE

Collaboration in each project phase, from pre-design through construction, has its own distinctive focus and feel. The essence of a traditional collaborative landscape is painted below in broad strokes: Scott Simpson, FAIA,[11] illustrates an ideal scene during construction that we can all emulate.

It's 2:00 pm sharp, and the project team is already assembled, ready to go. The owner, architect, consultants, and construction manager are all there— each a senior member of the team who is authorized to make decisions on the spot if needed. Everyone arrives on time. Cell phones are turned off, without a reminder, and there's hot coffee and water on a side table so that no one has to leave the room. On a large white board, the delivery date of the project is written in big, red letters: "February 28." Just below is a simple agenda with five bullet points outlining the key decisions that will be made during the course of the meeting. Off to one side is the "dinner box"—anyone who's available for a bite at the end of the day will check the box, and reservations will be booked before the meeting is over.

The agenda is quickly reviewed as the session begins, and then the team gets right to work. Item one: the contractor is having trouble fabricating the compound curvature for a wood stair rail, and wants to know what alternatives might be considered. Ideas are tossed back and forth freely among all the participants, covering aesthetics, materials, code requirements, cost, and schedule implications. After due consideration, the team decides to switch from wood to aluminum, which can be fabricated off site. Decision made. The team works the agenda until all five issues are covered. The meeting ends at 2:57 pm, with three minutes to spare. The time, place, and agenda for the next meeting are noted, and everyone leaves the room knowing what has to happen next to keep the project on track. By 9:00 am the next morning, meeting notes have been issued via email so that those who were not present know what to do. That night, five of the seven attendees make it for dinner, covering lots of napkins with sketches…

NOTES

1. Michael Schrage, *No More Teams: Mastering the Dynamics of Creative Collaboration*, New York: Currency/Doubleday, 1995, p. 33.

2. James C. McKinley Jr., "Hot Tracks, the Collaborative Method," *The New York Times*, February 9, 2012.

3. Roger Goldstein, personal communication with the author, November 3, 2008. FAIA—Fellow of the American Institute of Architects.

4. Scott Simpson, personal communication with the author, October 24, 2008.

5. Michael Schrage, *No More Teams: Mastering the Dynamics of Creative Collaboration*, New York: Currency/Doubleday, 1995, p. 46.

6. Ayn Rand, *The Fountainhead*, New York: The Bobbs-Merrill Company, 1943.

7. Tom Kelley with Jonathan Littman, *The Art of Innovation: Lessons in Creativity from IDEO, America's Leading Design Firm*, New York: Currency/Doubleday, 2001, p. 232.

8. Jim Summers, personal communication with the author, November 4, 2008.

9. Jerry Shea, "Building Prose for Building Pros," *Professional Practice 101: Business Strategies and Case Studies in Architecture*, Hoboken, NJ: John Wiley & Sons, 2006, p. 363. See the entire essay (pp. 361–366) for practical advice on how to write well.

10. Roger Fisher and William Ury, *Getting to Yes: Negotiating Agreement Without Giving In*, New York: Houghton Mifflin, 1981.

11. Scott Simpson, personal communication with the author, October 27, 2008.

Orchestrating active client collaboration together with the usual array of consultants from project inception is essential for creating beautiful and functional architecture. It is not possible for the architect to design in a vacuum with a unilateral effort and achieve a successful outcome (that is meaningful, useful, buildable, sustainable, and on budget and schedule). Incorporating ongoing, reciprocal dialogue with all stakeholders at all critical points during the design process and translating and integrating these data into the physical design is the only way a building can ultimately be considered successful.

The architect is the team member who has the unique creative talent—the training and experience to take an intuitive leap—to synthesize the data from other team members in a special way that drives the building design toward excellence. This assumes, obviously, that the architect has mastery of the requisite knowledge and skill set, and, of course, the facts of the specific project circumstances. In other words, the stage is set for a critical

2

ALTERNATIVE COLLABORATION MODELS FOR ARCHITECTURE

thought process whereby key information is focused upon, and irrelevant information is ignored. One part of the architect's responsibility is to educate the client about great design and show them exciting possibilities that they couldn't imagine—possibilities that are, naturally, based on the client's input. That is why the client is *not* an equal collaborator, even though they are a critically important part of the collaborative effort. Listening to the client is an absolute requirement. Translating, filtering, and inferring what the client says—not necessarily explicitly doing what the client says—is also an absolute requirement. Clients and other stakeholders can trigger ideas and inform design, but, alas, they are not designers. That's why there are architects. Stakeholder participation should be carefully limited and orchestrated to provide value to the design process depending on the sophistication and expertise of each stakeholder.

One of the issues with the conventional notion of all stakeholders—the entire design team—fully participating in the collaborative effort is that other than the architects, they are not trained or experienced in architectural design. This means that it is unlikely that they can contribute to the architectural vision in other than grandiose terms (however valuable that might be); they can't necessarily imagine what is possible. *Don't waste time* pursuing poor design ideas; this can be a big liability if the collaborative process is not managed well. On the other hand, stakeholders are essential in informing the development of the design—the parameters and the goals. And engineering consultants, constructors, product manufacturers, and so on are essential in implementing the magical concepts; some sort of innovation in their specialty area of expertise is usually necessary to arrive at the scheme proposed by the architect.

This discussion is not at all meant to suggest that "silos" of expertise be promoted. There is overlap in expertise, which must be incorporated into initial thinking about the project and development of concepts for truly integrated solutions. There are numerous examples of starting a project with an interdisciplinary charrette or workshop.

How collaborators participate in a project depends on the project circumstances and the consultants involved. As one of the first steps at project inception, the architect has to design the process, including the nature and frequency of interactions with consultants and others, taking into consideration his or her own capabilities with the technical issues. For example, the architect could have a conversation with the structural engineer and the sustainable design guru to inform the development of a concept. Perhaps there is a "deep dive" with a structural engineer but not the mechanical/electrical/plumbing engineers because of the nature of the project and the architect's comfort level with sustainable design issues. There might not be a reason to force a meeting with *every* consultant at *every* phase of the project.

Engineering consultants should not be regarded as mere technicians to execute a concept or squiggle by the architect in a silo, but as collaborators from project inception who are participants in a reciprocal dialogue at strategic points in the process to innovate, integrate, inform, and iterate. A traditionally minded engineer may have a certain conviction about collaboration. If the engineer has great talent, then consider designing and leading the process to harness that talent for the good of the project, even if it doesn't involve an enlightened view of collaboration.

Collaboration shouldn't be compromise. Compromise—the antithesis of synergy—will generally undermine the good ideas of a project and make its experience banal. Is it more courageous to listen and respond to the client and others on the design team, or to remain unyielding in standing behind some ideal, perfect creation? Or perhaps make the ideal, perfect creation *better* by absorbing and reinterpreting the critique?

MANAGED COLLABORATION: A NEW FRAMEWORK FOR THE DESIGN PROCESS

Building on the discussions and definition of collaboration in Chapter 1, the notion of "managed collaboration" and its specific application to architecture and construction can now be fully illuminated. In general terms then, managed collaboration is a proposal for an inclusive process that informs and enriches a design project; that optimizes contributions from the participants in synergistic fashion. It is an aggressive, project-specific method of deploying a full collaboration mode at various integration points when consultant teams come together. The architect designs a process of inquiry for each project and set of team members.

The trajectory of a managed collaborative process can be viewed as a rapid evolution through time marked by a series of inputs from consultant teams that represent the involved specialties. At each input from a specialty, the architect faces an integrative challenge, i.e. to wed the specialist's work gracefully with the work on a project to date in a manner consistent with, and complementary to, the overall concept.

In this manner, specialized and talented teams working independently provide highly focused, substantive and innovative pieces of the whole. Joining, massaging, and refining the sequentially contributed pieces from each team in a manner consistent with the overarching mission or concept becomes the responsibility of the architect who manages the collaborative process. Any managed process is intended to enhance efficiency and lower costs by controlling or manipulating as many variables as possible in a manner that accelerates pace and minimizes redundancy and waste.

It is perhaps counterintuitive, but personality and politics are thus minimized and creativity and efficiency are optimized since there is in effect a reduction of competing noise from "too many cooks." Rather than an entire orchestra of contributors, a project leader or manager is freed to critically appraise, distill, and assemble the independently developed components.

This managed process (see Figure 2.1) is a model of professional collaboration that places the architect in a more authoritative and also more creative position. Ideas, not ideology or personality, become the focus. Individual specialty teams collaborate actively among themselves but not across teams—except during integration points. Again, intervening variables, potential obstructions, or delays in the design or idea-development process are minimized with personality and politics less prominent since the evolution of the project through time is shepherded by a single individual. In the absence of noise or frank interference arising inevitably from competing voices or ideas from each specialty team, the architect is given a greater opportunity to see more clearly and precisely how specialty inputs may fit with or reinforce the design concept.

It is intriguing to explore application of this style of collaborative process to any professional endeavor. This approach already exists in medicine to a degree, with

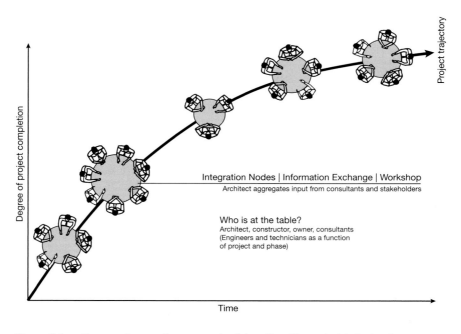

Integration Nodes | Information Exchange | Workshop
Architect aggregates input from consultants and stakeholders

Who is at the table?
Architect, constructor, owner, consultants
(Engineers and technicians as a function
of project and phase)

Figure 2.1   Process diagram for managed collaboration. The project trajectory is characterized by a series of inputs from consultant teams that are managed and led by the architect. Workshops can be an inspiring way to advance the project at integration nodes (see Chapter 4 for details).

its specialty or consultation focus in responsive service to the internal medicine or surgical attending physician. Within architecture, there are the routine instances of consultation by structural, mechanical, and civil engineers, etc. The leap in the present conception lies with the understanding or assumption that the architect serves as a relatively freewheeling evaluator and integrator of ideas provided by the component specialty teams. The architect arrives at a design concept in the earliest phase of the project, but thereafter serves primarily to assure that the specialty teams produce work consistent with that concept. Collaboration involves a focus on ideas, on the marriage of the work of specialty teams to a dynamic integrative process, which occurs periodically at nodes of integration and finally at the "executive" level of the architect. Competing personalities and personal agendas, then, are necessarily of less prominence.

Team members will have to accept specific direction about where they can contribute, and live with an architect-leader who will be assertive and even autocratic. Collaboration in the present conception is directed by an aggressive, prominent exercise of leadership. The empowered leader deploys the collaborators at exactly the right time and place to minimize redundancy, noise, clashing person-alities—versus the traditional model of collaboration in which collaborators are bound by mutual obligations and personal relationships. It may well be a challenge for team members and consultants to accept and participate in a managed system as characterized here; expectations for personal and professional behavior will inevi-tably favor those who are more comfortable functioning independently and without the traditional crosstalk and continual interaction with some proximate matrix of colleagues. In fact, it is arguable that the "virtual" office in which principals work in relative isolation and electronically transmit their work to some central integrative point is the optimal framework for a managed approach to collaboration.

How does the architect deal with many voices trying to contribute at the same time or in random fashion, as in a brainstorming or charrette session? The answer is that the architect designs and diagrams when and how team members participate. In contrast to the constant ebb and flow of discussion and feedback, much of which is of little consequence, the architect can schedule creative and problem-solving sessions in which focus and yield are maximized.

In a strictly managed framework, then, the architect would be empowered to break down silos to most efficiently support a project. This model of collaboration works when specialties are guided as if by an orchestra conductor. The architect does not allow the collaborative activity to happen naturally; the leader makes it happen as a function of what is important at that specific point in the project, and for advancing the project. This approach is optimally cost and time effective. *The architect becomes a designer and manager of the process—as much as he or she may be manager of the project.*

The architect clearly defines the process of working together, which is admittedly different for each project (as a function of scale, budget, stakeholders, etc.). For example, creative tracks can be identified, each of which has a specialty leader. A diagram of when the tracks cross (and how long [time] and how thick [scope of work] they are) serves to illustrate integration nodes and the extent of a given specialty's input relative to the whole project. But for every project, project goals and more global agendas of team members are upfront and center. Collaborative activity can best be framed as a design problem; list the variables. Consultants have varying degrees of immersion; the architect must limit or increase participation as a function of project and design requirements. Identify when to apply focused team effort—anywhere from a large inclusive team to small deep dive. Scale the team to the specific task.

In a managed practice, the architect's relationship with the consultants is *not* reciprocal. Alas, there is little time and money to entertain their input on architectural design issues (unless you want to cut profit). There is great respect for their expertise, but not necessarily for their architectural design. As the architect, imagine how you would discuss the project with consultants; elicit their feedback related to their area of expertise and how that will influence the design. The architect must facilitate the consultants' dialogue with each other—for example, when the structural engineer needs to talk with the mechanical engineer. In that case the architect directs the structural engineer to take the lead in that discussion.

The concept of managed practice addresses the architects' primal fear of losing control—or, more important, diluting his or her great ideas—in a collaborative model of practice. In this model, however, they are thrust into a transcendent and very creative role; that is, directing, integrating, driving, and harvesting ideas in support of the concept—and ensuring its integrity.

PRECEDENTS FOR MANAGED COLLABORATION FROM OTHER DISCIPLINES

Collaborative practice has played a significant role in many other professions and industries. Examining managed collaborative practice in other fields can yield fresh insights into the prospective benefits of this process in architectural practice.

A dramatic illustration of managed collaboration comes from the aviation industry. The Airbus Industries A380 airliner is a breathtaking achievement in aircraft design and construction. In 1999, the European aircraft manufacturer Airbus initiated the A380 project to manufacture the world's first truly double-decker airliner with a theoretical high-density passenger seating capacity of more than 800. Airbus adopted what is considered a revolutionary decentralized manufacturing process.

The centers that manufactured various parts were arrayed across Europe, and the final assembly was completed at Toulouse, France, under the watchful eyes of a handful of project managers who possessed *absolute authority*. State-of-the-art composites that reduced the overall weight of the aircraft were used to optimize the strength-to-weight ratio, which in turn revolutionized fuel economy and range.

Collaboration involving high technology at a large scale is a very different entity from a traditional model. "Family" no longer provides the effective and efficient matrix. During World War II, 2,751 Liberty Ships were constructed in four years! This feat required partnerships among specialties that broke new ground in shipbuilding, which were, in turn, *directed almost exclusively by one individual,* Henry J. Kaiser.

Other seminal examples of managed collaboration include the Skunk Works founded in 1943 and the Manhattan Project founded in 1941 in which conflicts were notorious, with *many more physicists than team builders.* In each instance, the huge talents and huge egos were minimized, integrated, and melded into a synergy by a handful of strong leaders who identified a clear task and timetable and made certain the project adhered to and achieved the goals. In the case of the Manhattan Project, J. Robert Oppenheimer was endowed with autocratic power by project leader, General Leslie Groves. Groves was an experienced manager who had overseen the construction of the Pentagon; he was described as pushy and overbearing but his organizational and managerial acumen drove the Manhattan Project ahead of similar German and Russian efforts.

At Lockheed's Skunk Works, which closed in 1990, Kelly Johnson worked for more than four decades as the organizing genius, design authority, and aggressive manager. He designed and/or contributed to the development of more than 40 revolutionary aircraft. The first of his "Fourteen Rules of Management" was: "The Skunk Works manager must be delegated practically complete control of his program in all aspects."[1]

Also consider the Apollo Project (1961–1972). Some 400,000 people and 20,000 firms and universities were wrapped up in the effort; but a handful, in fact arguably three or four, administrators and managers are credited with shaping and directing the entire program and its historic result. The essence of managed collaboration is networking or connecting actors with others in some algorithmic matrix that supports focused productivity quickly and effectively while providing a single authoritative vision that creates common ground among what may be a diverse set of stake-holders and the creative products of their effort.

There is a synergy in collaboration that is nothing short of a powerful force multiplier. The common denominator among the examples above revealed by temporal analysis of the planning and design processes is sequential integration of the work of discrete and talented teams facilitated and directed by, at most, only a few individuals.

Another way of conceptualizing a rational managed collaborative model might be to view it as the anatomy of wiring in the human brain. In 2011, IBM announced it created a series of prototype chips "designed to emulate the brain's abilities for perception, action, and cognition."[2] It is an elegant and clean plan in which the various functions are all equally weighted and each depends on the others. Invoking terms and models inspired by neuroscience, the chips use digital silicon circuits to construct a "neurosynaptic core" or executive operating system with integrated memory (replicated synapses), computational power (replicated neurons), and communication (replicated axons). This template can be readily extended to a model of collaboration that mimics the brain's logic, efficiency, and power. Sensory inputs can be equated with inputs from specialty teams—the various engineering consultants, landscape architects, interior designers, cost estimators, and so on. The architect's neurosynaptic core then processes and creatively integrates the specialty inputs, which then inform a design via replicated axonal networks.

Of course, what is glaringly absent in the IBM model are structural entities for (1) leadership or superego, and (2) emotion along with its means of connection with all the other components. These may represent the elusive or magical factors— inspiration, passion, motivation, sentiment, mood, integration, and personality/ coping style—all the purposeful and affective variables that make up the contri- bution to any and all human endeavors. Analysis of emotion plays more readily into a discussion of leadership than collaboration, which will be elaborated under "Leading collaborative projects" in Chapter 3. For the present focus on the structure of collaboration, the emotional factors are subservient to the architecture of the collaborative network.

AN INTEGRATED APPROACH TO COLLABORATION

This section examines an approach to collaboration that integrates aspects of tradi- tional and managed models by applying a model from the realm of government and political science. The discussion will explore the notions of a *traditional* "confeder- ation" and the more *managed* "federation" in which individual member components (i.e. the states) operate separately from, yet are integrally part of a (federal) whole under some executive leadership.

In other words, a confederation is a means of unifying an alliance that consoli- dates authority from other autonomous (or semi-autonomous) bodies in support of common action. In contrast, in a federation, the component states are in some sense sovereign, but far greater powers and control reside with the central leadership (representing the managed side of collaborative practice).

The character and degree of central leadership and influence of the federation differs from case to case. Cases differ essentially in terms of how much control rests with the leader. In any case, there is a dynamic give-and-take between the executive leadership and the component "states." Each state has its own resources, initiatives, and leadership that are to some degree aligned with, and supportive of, the overarching priorities and goals of the federal whole.

Strictly federal (managed) leadership assures coordination and forward movement, which may arise even out of chaos and fragmentation. Greater executive or central power and authority pushes confederation toward the pole of "federation."

CONFEDERATION VS. FEDERATION: TRADITIONAL VS. MANAGED STYLES

In a metaphor for professional practice, the members of the confederation are specialty teams and consultants (which comprise the bulk of the resources and capacity for design production). The leadership function is assumed by the principal architect. The tone is likely to be more traditionally cooperative and interactive. If the lead architect invokes and applies aspects of a "managed" style consistent with "federation," the tone becomes more directive and even autocratic. In each instance, in order to optimize process and fit firm function to client and project requirements, the leader makes a considered determination about style of practice.

THE INTEGRATED APPROACH

In football parlance, with the integrated model, the more successful game manager or quarterback is able to "call an audible." After "reading" the defensive scheme arrayed in front of him and taking careful account of position on the field, weather and turf conditions, and his team's strengths and weaknesses, the quarterback may need to adjust or change a predesigned play. At the line of scrimmage, the quarterback must be willing to, and able to, throw or run the ball downfield. This metaphor establishes a project leader as an "option quarterback" of sorts, able to adjust their leadership style and the way in which their team functions according to the specific realities and challenges of the moment. The integrated model then becomes an implicit challenge and mandate to professional practice education.

If any of the models of some collaborative evolution or ideal in architecture are to become useful devices, they must be well defined and tested in some meaningful and systematic fashion. It might be argued that an economically safe incubator or laboratory could exist in the schools of architecture. In the face of economic adversity and change, the educational lab may be an optimal environment in which a practice simulation can be conceived and tested. Moreover, the opportunity may exist to give birth to a new and authentic leadership culture among students and influentials alike. Alternatively and perhaps more realistically, trials within large firms might be initiated more readily. Apart from the prospective benefit for practice, such efforts within and outside of the academy might serve to catalyze and sustain innovation.

A purely managed style of leadership is clearly a simpler approach; it is, in fact, almost algorithmic, and favors application by leaders who are less comfortable with that "option quarterback" style noted above. The likely efficiency and impact of the managed approach has been amply demonstrated in other fields, as reviewed in Chapter 3. In the more complex and creative sphere of architectural work, the collision of ethical and legal obligations, regulatory controls, building performance standards, planning exigencies, and client and employee satisfaction issues may render the traditional approach ineffectual and inefficient. While the algorithmic managed approach may seem to be a potent and efficient strategy for driving a project from conception to completion, it may fail in the very quixotic, psychosocial, and technical soup of the architectural enterprise. In contrast, the integrated model offers the possibility of hybridizing both the soft-and-gentle traditional style and the hard-and-fast managed style. The skilled leader would be enabled to blend the loosely organized, purely collaborative webs within and outside a firm with occasional directive, autocratic helmsmanship.

The logical extension of any discussion about an emerging or novel concept involves not only the issue of proof-of-concept in the practice setting, and curriculum in the educational sphere, but also, unavoidably, applications of the social media movement. In the present discussion, the potential of online gaming as a consciousness-raising or educational aid cannot be overstated. From team sports simulation to disaster management, online video games offer astonishing opportunities both for enter-tainment and training, not to mention profit for the sponsoring agency. One can imagine the AIA promoting a "Masters of Design" game in which participants engage a client, define user groups, analyze a site, and generate a program for a building type they then design with input from various consultants. Challenges in terms of design problems, environmental exigencies, budgetary constraints, difficult person-alities, conflicts among specialist consultants, technical glitches, and problems with subcontractors and constructors can all be simulated with sophisticated but now routinely produced graphics power and animation. Success in the game can be defined by choices that lead to creation of a well-functioning, visually appealing, and "green" building that satisfies client, building users, and the community. Decisions involving project phasing, coordination, late modifications to the design, conflict management, and other issues that may arise in the project's trajectory can also be readily gamed, and present rich learning opportunities.

LEADERSHIP WITHIN AN INTEGRATED APPROACH

According to Fred Fiedler,[3] there is no ideal leader. In his typology, "task-oriented" and "relationship-oriented" leaders can be effective if their leadership orientation fits the situation. Extending this proposition in terms of a "traditional" vs. "managed" approach to facilitating or leading a collaborative endeavor in practice, it is not a stretch to begin to develop the theoretical basis for an "integrated" style. Fiedler's theory allows for a well-resolved description of the elements of such a style:

1. **Leader–Member Relations**, referring to the degree of mutual trust, respect and confidence between the leader and the subordinates.

2. **Task Structure**, referring to the extent to which group tasks are clear and structured.

3. **Leader Position Power**, referring to the power inherent in the leader's position itself.

When there is a good leader–member relationship and a clearly structured set of tasks, a "traditional" style may be optimal. With very high leader position power and a complex and widespread task structure, a "managed" style may be ideal. In the language I have been invoking, leader–situation match and mismatch would then dictate the optimal collaborative style. Since personality is relatively stable, Fiedler's model suggests that improving effectiveness requires modifying the situation to fit the leader. This he calls "job engineering" or "job restructuring," and it may not be applicable or even possible in the context of an architectural project. In this instance, the firm or the leader may make adjustments to task structure, formal position power, and chain of command.

Strictly task-oriented or managed leadership would be appropriate to leading teams responding to a disaster requiring an immediate and multi-level response, such as an earthquake or flu pandemic. In an uncertain space, leader–member relations are typically and necessarily one-dimensional and minimalist, and the task is highly complex and fluid. The successful leader usually has a strong and even charismatic/therapeutic presence, but does not know subordinates personally. The task-oriented leader who gets things accomplished usually emerges as the most effective. If the leader is "traditionally" considerate (relationship-oriented), critical time may be wasted while disaster-associated events escalate.

The traditional (relationship-oriented) style may be optimal in an environment where the situation is more benign and well delineated. Clearly there is some self-selection in the movement of leaders with their unique styles toward firms with practices that may best match that style, but it is certainly not always the case. Recognition of very specific flavors of collaborative leadership—or design of relationships—is an important step in a conscious effort to engineer them in support of more effective and efficient practice. Whether we alter our styles of leadership to promote a superior fit with firm personnel and projects, or recruit leaders whose personalities better match the situational reality, we at least recognize the significance of the spectrum of professional collaboration.

NOTES

1. "Kelly's 14 Rules & Practices," Lockheed Martin, www.lockheedmartin.com/us/aeronautics/skunkworks/14rules.html (accessed April 29, 2013).

2. Brad Chacos, "IBM Creates Cognitive Chips Modeled After The Human Brain," *Maximum PC Magazine*, August 18, 2011, online edition, www.maximumpc.com/article/news/ibm_creates_cognitive_chips_modeled_after_human_brain.

3. Fred E. Fiedler, Martin M. Chemers, and Linda Mahar, *Improving Leadership Effectiveness: The Leader Match Concept*, New York: John Wiley & Sons, 1976.

In contrast to a managed collaborative process, the value of a more traditional form of collaborative practice is worth reviewing, especially in the context of the current workplace trend that allows flexibility to work remotely from home and telecommute rather than work in an office. There are a number of companies, however, that are resisting that trend including Yahoo, Google, Facebook, Zappos, and other tech companies. The feeling is that there is rarely a substitute for face-to-face collaboration as a way to innovate. It was reported that Yahoo recently abolished its work-at-home policy. In making the announcement, Jackie Reses,[1] director of human resources, stated in the company's memo, "Some of the best decisions and insights come from hallway and cafeteria discussions, meeting new people and impromptu team meetings. Speed and quality are often sacrificed when we work from home." Indeed, leadership and firm culture—discussed in this chapter—are important aspects of fostering a traditional collaborative mindset.

3

TRADITIONAL COLLABORATION IN PRACTICE

LEADING COLLABORATIVE PROJECTS

We're talking about somebody's life here. We can't decide it in five minutes. …
We nine can't understand how you three are still so sure. Maybe you can tell us.

Henry Fonda as a juror in 12 Angry Men[2]

With just two brief quotes from this 1957 film classic, Henry Fonda's character—an architect—begins to emerge as the leader of a group of men who are deciding a capital murder case. He is the lone dissenter initially but eventually is able to persuade the other 11 jurors to revisit the evidence and acquit the suspect on the basis of reasonable doubt. His successful strategies for leading the group include encouraging equal and inclusive participation and taking time to deliberate slowly. He listens carefully and considers the varying agendas of the other jurors without judgment so he can understand their perspectives, proffer new ideas persuasively, and then influence the outcome.

While life-and-death decisions are not usually part of an architect's daily routine, and collaborative teams are not normally as unruly as that jury was, architects who are capable leaders hold great power. Appropriately applying that power to lead a collaborative design team and direct efforts to integrate the work of all of the consultants into a synergistic whole can result in innovative and creative architecture.

How should the architect lead and mobilize the team to move the project forward, to complete the next steps to the highest degree of excellence? The conventional approach is framed by the question, "I know the right thing to do, now how can I learn how to collaborate with people so I can get them to do what I want them to do?" A better question, however, for leading a high-powered, multidisciplinary team is, "I have some thoughts about what we should do, how can I effectively share my insights and what I care about with others while also authentically listening to their insights?" This suggests an attitude about leadership and collaboration, one that requires enough wisdom to know that someone else may have an even better idea.[3]

Architects are trained to think critically and go beyond the status quo to form meaningful new ideas. This unique skill set and expertise gives them the ability to see the big picture, reframe questions to see different perspectives, create innovative design solutions to problems, attend to detail, manage and reconcile diverse and complex interests—and relationships. Architects who possess these skills, which are also characteristics of great leaders in other disciplines, can leverage these insights to lead effectively. Many architects have just the right background to lead.

Exposing staff at all levels in the firm to clients and consultants as often as possible can be an effective approach to leading teams in addition to cultivating leadership

Figure 3.1   Henry Fonda plays an architect in the film *12 Angry Men,* the story of a jury deciding the fate of a man on trial for murder. Initially, his is the sole vote against a conviction but eventually—in a demonstration of great leadership— he is able to persuade the other jurors to reexamine the evidence and acquit on the basis of reasonable doubt. (Photo by United Artists/Courtesy of Getty Images.)

from the ranks. This is a powerful way for staff to understand client and consultant perspectives, and why the principals are leading the project in a certain fashion. If staff hear it directly from the client, they are more likely to become truly invested in the project, which facilitates collaboration. The essence of this leadership style is to engage the office with clients and consultants to impart the values—and reap the rewards—of teamwork. One of the goals of this strategy, then, is to develop, among all team members, the ability to listen intently to clients from the very start when they express what they need their project to do for them.[4] This is analogous to a clinical or therapeutic approach to leading a team.

Numerous surveys indicate that architects are highly respected in our culture. Maybe that aura is what made Henry Fonda's juror so influential. Regardless, it could translate into enormous potential for reaching large multidisciplinary teams including clients, community members, and other stakeholders who may not always be receptive. Inspired and dynamic leaders embrace change, listen well, articulate their vision, motivate, think critically and creatively, reflect, prioritize, and then act.

LEADERSHIP BASICS

Traditional collaboration requires truly great leadership in addition to someone who is ultimately responsible for making decisions.

Given knowledgeable and responsible problem solvers, the architect-leader must free the team member to plug whatever creative talent they have into the collaborative process. You can't orchestrate the making of magic but you must set the stage to let it happen. The leader is in essence a teacher who has the ability to push and pull, critique, improvise, and use significant amounts of intuition to advance the project.

What are the three most important tools for architect-leaders?

1. **Donuts and coffee.** In many different contexts, these tools facilitate face-to-face sessions to build goodwill, rapport, respect, and an understanding of positions. Don't underestimate the power of the donut in breaking down barriers of all types.

2. **Thick markers and tracing paper.** Architects have a huge advantage in leading and working collaboratively because they can use the language of drawing to inspire, create, and communicate with others. Leverage this skill; use it as often as possible.

3. **Ongoing and frequent dialogue.** Dialogue, both collectively and individually in a range of media, is essential for engagement and inclusion, which leads to investment in the work. Effective dialogue means that a good leader listens well and continually motivates to advance the project.

In the traditional model of collaboration, the architect assumes responsibility for leading the whole process, responding in varied ways as a function of the project and the team, but also focusing on engagement with the team at all levels and on a personal as well as professional basis. Being the architect on a project means you have the vision and purpose, set the tone, create the concepts, understand the context, engage and direct the consultants and inspire them with the vision, and know how to reach the end result. What follows are some basic leadership tips.

- Listen carefully to team members and have frequent one-on-one face-to-face conversations. This is how a genuine connection is established and sustained. This is by far the best way to communicate important information, and to direct the individual's talent to the work of the project. Take full advantage of media that promote an exchange of ideas. This exchange must be reciprocal so that the team member can express passion for the project and the ideas will flow. Arrange meetings between various select players as needed for coordination and integration; then the larger team meetings may be more focused and effective.

- Provide explicit goals, expectations, and roles for both the team as a whole and each collaborator. Then, as the project evolves, figure out how to inspire each team member.

- Demonstrate how, and ensure, that individual team members feel that their input was helpful in advancing the project.

- Be decent and responsible when giving critical feedback. Be constructive and positive. Don't be judgmental, at least initially. Avoiding exclusively negative feedback—for example, by instead suggesting exploration of specific alternatives—can preserve self-confidence, and help to elicit a more creative contribution. Be mindful that all team members are in this together, including the leader.

- Nurture the best in each diverse personality. Reach out and connect with each individual as a unique and valued member of the team.

- Be a resource for the team. Serve the team rather than rule as a dictator. Provide support. Educate, encourage, facilitate strengths and mitigate weaknesses to the extent possible.

- Be a role model for the team. Establish and demonstrate work habits, professionalism (i.e. engage team members with respect and appreciation), fairness, lead from the front (no task is too menial), and be authentic.

- Be persistent in trying to inspire and develop innovative ideas. Reframe architectural ideas to allow collaborators (especially consultants) to apply their own specialized expertise to the problem.

- Allow others to lead at certain times, as circumstances suggest.

- Diagram team members' characteristics, especially their strengths, to assist in broadly suggesting roles. Be cognizant of and then direct how collaborators can bring their unique, creative expertise and potential to bear on the project.

- Design interventions as appropriate to keep the project on track—from nuanced suggestions to audacious proposals.

- Genuinely care about those under your leadership. Ensure that everyone has an opportunity to meaningfully contribute, learn, and grow.

DECISION-MAKING

Ironically, successful collaboration almost always requires some degree of autocratic leadership. No ambiguity about it, the architect, as leader, must be empowered to make final decisions, while occasionally deferring to expert specialists. Openness to alternatives at every phase is implicit in this model. Nevertheless, a team leader or champion must be identified early on, and it must be agreed that final authority rests with that individual. Sarah Harkness,[5] one of the original partners with Walter Gropius of The Architects Collaborative, has quoted Gropius as proclaiming that to "safeguard design coherence and impact, the right of making final decisions must be left exclusively to the one member who happens to be responsible for a specific job, even though his decision should run counter to the opinion of other members." The point is that one way to avoid either endless, unproductive discussion or the cliché, "a camel is a horse designed by committee," is to have a leader who is empowered to make informed decisions after listening to, understanding, and appreciating the perspectives from all team members.

A hybrid approach to making decisions can be useful depending on the specific nature of what is being decided (and the time frame) during the course of a project. For example, the leader can defer to an expert, there can be discussion and consensus, or the leader can make an informed unilateral decision, as described above.

EGO MANAGEMENT

Orchestration of a collaborative work session usually involves a complex and subtle manipulation on the part of leadership so that the inevitably talented and distinctive personalities that make up a team may interact positively and productively. Management of healthy egos is a priority because it is not always realistic, possible, or even desirable to follow the conventional wisdom that egos must be checked at the door. Participants must believe they can do the impossible in order to *do* the impossible and innovate.

It behooves the leader to simultaneously encourage individual participation and "foster an environment where the team owns ideas, rather than each member owning his or her own," says Morris A. Nunes,[6] a Fairfax, Virginia, attorney who represents practices and privately held businesses. He underscores that the team should be coached, nurtured, and incentivized as a team. In other words, every collaborator works for the good of the project—and shares the rewards as well as the risks. Nunes claims that Ben Franklin's famous quote, "We must all hang together or we shall surely hang separately," should be a constant refrain.

LEADERSHIP WITH A LIGHT TOUCH AND SHARING POWER

Some degree of hierarchy and authority is necessary even in the most democratic collaborative groups. There must be a distinct leader who keeps the team focused and directs decision-making. Totally free-form approaches may waste precious energy, time, and money, and in the long run, may sew the seeds for further anarchistic impediments. However, there is certainly a light touch to leading teams at Gensler. Jordan Goldstein,[7] AIA, Managing Director of the Washington, DC office, describes their team leaders as "facilitators and conductors of the larger symphony, which includes the design team, client, contractor, consultants, and vendors." The leader is frequently the one who initiated the client relationship. He says that Gensler aims to have horizontal team structures in which every team member is contributing to decision-making so that it is not being delayed by levels of internal bureaucracy.

Leading by example—demonstrating how to be a good team member and team leader—is an important ingredient for success. Morris Nunes[8] succinctly underscores the message: "The overall tone must be set from the top and must be lived and embraced day to day as part of an organization's culture. When an organization's leaders are successful in inculcating that spirit, teamwork becomes second nature." As the leader, make sure you are visible so team members can observe how you behave collaboratively; for example, let others listen-in on phone conversations and sit-in on meetings to see how you communicate in action.

FOSTERING COLLABORATION

Basic consideration and kindness preserve goodwill and self-esteem of the individuals on the team. A great leader should be able to reference one individual's valuable comments and how they may complement another's and, in this way promote, even *coerce* collaboration. Self-conscious but genuine appreciation of the contributions of each team member bolsters confidence and is crucial to sustaining effective and efficient process and outcome. Specific invitation to each team member to modify, challenge, even offer starkly contrasting alternatives to the consensus goes a long way in supporting a team's capacity to drive an evolving synthesis of ideas.

COLLABORATION AS FUN

Humor, shared meals, gatherings or retreats in places other than the office, and team work-outs are all strategies for injecting some enjoyment and novelty into the work routines. The associated team building will also result in enhanced team cohesion, collective self-esteem, and efficiency in breaking down barriers to collaboration. Picture a group of 11 or 12 men and women on mountain bikes, peddling in smaller groups of two or three. They are all brainstorming about a particularly challenging problem of creating a structural system that will literally and figuratively support an architectural concept. Don't underestimate the value of having fun as an integral part of the collaborative process; it may promote better understanding of each other's perspectives, diffuse tension and stress—making it easier to address conflicts, and in general promote an esprit de corps.

THE ART OF WORKING WITH DIFFICULT TEAM MEMBERS

Take time to discuss a problem one-on-one and face-to-face to get the individual on board as an ally. Examine the issue objectively and make an appeal for a *fair* analysis. Acknowledge the difficulties and inevitabilities of conflict among distinctive and talented personalities. Offer concrete examples of approaches to managing clashes. Relate similar situations that you personally encountered and managed with varying degrees of success or failure. Revealing and freely recounting failures can be a very effective means of connecting with employees and colleagues and developing trust and respect.

View resolving conflicts as a design problem. Most problems are survivable, negotiable, and may even constitute an opportunity. Relationships that endure tough start-up may turn out to be the most gratifying and meaningful. One approach that has stood the test of time is to effect a self-effacing posture, and ask for help, suggestions, or guidance based on the other person's legitimate experience and achievement. In other words, diffuse the chip-on-the-shoulder by making it into a helper and mentor. Incorporating suggestions, even at the expense of some of your own ideas, is likely to serve you well—and you may learn something too. Development of more genuine personal bonds is then facilitated, and with the passage of time, it will be easier to disagree without emotional or professional cost.

Reinterpreting antagonistic questions and comments to promote analysis can be a graceful tactic. Tension can be diffused and progress can be restored by yielding to, or acknowledging a critical or confrontational barb.

THE ART OF BEING A GOOD TEAM MEMBER

Effective team members tend to (1) be passionate about the work and of course enjoy doing it and derive satisfaction from it; (2) know what they are doing, at least possessing a mastery of the basics (fundamental knowledge and skills) plus the ability and desire to learn; and (3) possess a warm and outgoing personality.

Everyone must make the collaborative process their own to some degree in order to perform best and achieve magical results. There must be a cognizance of the issues involved in collaborating in any given case. Motivation is very important to understand. As a professional, you are obligated to care for other people. The first people you care for are the people sitting next to you. There is a brotherhood that is based on the principle of caring for other people—part of the definition of architecture as one of the great service professions. Architecture as a profession, more than any other, combines creativity and beauty as well as technology in taking care of clients as people, as part of a society, as part of a public in shaping the environment.

Idealism, e.g. to save the environment and the planet, is the sort of noble intention that drives architects toward excellence. That kind of ambition—striving to do important things—can inspire and motivate every team member.

The architecture mission is noble, professional, and includes: creation of magical, poetic, functional, high-performance buildings; serving the clients/owners/users; and training/mentoring/role modeling of young practitioners. All of this must be intertwined while doing the work; these components are not separate and distinct. The traditional conventions for participating on the architectural team include the following:

- First, recognize that the project will benefit from a collaborative effort; and second, that you *want* to participate in such an effort.

- Each team member must be committed to the success of all of the other team members, especially when there are issues of coordination and overlap.

- Each team member must be committed to the success of the project above all else (invoke the "why are you an architect?" question). Be unpretentious and willing to respond positively to critical feedback for the good of the project.

- Be courageous. Don't hesitate to take a position and disagree with other team members, the leader, and client in support of a good idea that will benefit the project.

- Temporarily assume a leadership role when circumstances suggest it, i.e. your special expertise will be driving decisions and project direction.

- Don't be shy about developing and presenting new ideas for appraisal by collaborators.

- "Don't confuse routine with commitment."[9]

FIRM CULTURE TO FACILITATE COLLABORATION

Cultivating an environment in which there is a swift and easy exchange of ideas is an important part of the collaborative design process in many firms, both large and small. What may not be so obvious are strategies to foster optimal functioning and creative thinking in such a team-oriented environment.

Early in their indoctrination and training, architecture students learn about design studio culture. Architecture schools are required to demonstrate a healthy design studio culture in order to be accredited, and criteria include encouraging "respect, engagement, and innovation among faculty and student body,"[10] which should serve as a model of professional conduct in the future.

There is increasing recognition that a firm's cultural environment is a critical factor not only in producing the best possible design work but also in attracting and retaining both new staff and clients. Many architectural firms are now including sections on their websites dedicated to describing a distinctive office culture. Their intent is to demonstrate that the firm has a climate in which excellent design can be nurtured, so they can serve as a magnet for talented people, who are always in great demand.

By definition, the design process involves some degree of innovation relative to a unique set of project circumstances. Since design—and its management—is the core of what most architects do, it follows that creating the environment to facilitate an innovative subculture that promotes collaboration should likewise be a main concern.

A firm's culture, as succinctly characterized by Jean Valence, Hon AIA,[11] "encompasses its history and accomplishments, its leaders' ambitions and goals, its definition of and criteria for excellence, its attitude about clients and staff, its traditions and lore, its mood and energy, and its balance between art and business." In other words, a firm's values describe its culture, and the subcultural components such as those promoting collaboration, innovation, continuing education, communication, and so on, impart a distinct personality.

STRATEGIES THAT SUPPORT A SUBCULTURE OF INNOVATION AND COLLABORATION

Here are a few strategies suggested by experts to encourage innovation and collaboration that might surprise you: Hire naive misfits who argue with you; encourage failure; avoid letting client input limit your vision; and fully commit to risky ventures. This is an extreme approach to fostering innovation and collaboration in an otherwise relatively static office environment that was proposed by Robert I. Sutton.[12] Sutton argued that fresh perspectives derive from mavericks with wildly diverse backgrounds and no preconceptions who challenge the status quo, champion their own ideas, and illuminate the metaphorical darkness.

Sutton points out that ignoring client input, for example, may seem counterintuitive but clients can't always imagine what's possible. Likewise, failure is critical to the design process—assuming the team learns from the failure—because, typically, many bad ideas must be generated to produce a terrific one. Even the bad ideas can illuminate a problem and serve as a creative trigger to its solution.

A somewhat more tempered and time-proven model of Sutton's dogma is embodied in the culture of the United States Navy. The role of the executive officer, or second-in-command, is historically charged with such principles as support and delegation of authority. But also implicit is the responsibility of providing alternative, even self-consciously innovative, solutions to problems that may arise in battle or in other emergency situations. Frankly opposite viewpoints from those of the commanding officer are often invited and seen as requisite components of tactical decision-making. The resulting complementary tension that exists between the commanding and executive officers is considered a positive force that enriches the culture because it demands that alternative strategies must be considered. Perhaps a formalized notion of a second-in-command equivalent that would add some creative and energetic tension could be a beneficial addition to some architecture firms' cultures, improving the underlying process and dynamic of their design teams' collaborative efforts.

The notion of a council of experts made up of senior members of a practice, as a resource that contributes to a learning environment through mentoring, supporting teams and individuals with new ideas, and sharing best practices, is a powerful cultural attribute. Moreover, tapping into a firm's internal expertise can assist design teams in understanding particular building types and technologies in an accelerated manner.

LOOK OUTSIDE FOR INSIGHT

Applying cross-disciplinary knowledge to help creatively solve architectural problems—and broaden perspectives—is a time-honored strategy. The Seattle firm Olson Kundig Architects[13] employs a visiting lecturer series, which, according to its website, is "inspired by the power of cross-fertilization—where individuals who excel in disciplines other than architecture come and share with us what they do." They have had presentations by artists, craftspeople, environmentalists, and even an exotic dancer.

Reorganizing staff can fuel new approaches to engaging everyday problems. Roger Goldstein, FAIA,[14] a Principal at Goody Clancy in Boston, explains that intentionally mixing teams from one project to the next is an integral part of his firm's culture. He says, "There's a lot of value in applying the things we learn in one realm to another completely different context." There is, however, a delicate balance in composing a team with experts in a particular building type (that appeals to prospective clients) and those with little experience who come to the table with no preconceptions, contribute fresh ideas, and challenge basic assumptions. "Team composition that might lead to the most efficient design process does not necessarily lead to the best design," explains Goldstein.

"One way for a majority of staff to have a degree of ownership in the design process," claims Michael Ryan,[15] Principal of Environmental Dynamics Inc. (EDI), Albuquerque, "is to sponsor a group charrette for larger projects in which everyone gets to draw and design in the schematic phase." Roger Goldstein similarly believes that charging a design team to spend a few days developing a number of ideas that may or may not be workable is not only intriguing for pushing the design envelope but contributes to a culture of innovation.

Does everything have to be touchy-feely in traditional collaboration? Are competition and collaboration within the same firm culture mutually exclusive? Not according to IDEO founder David Kelly.[16] He describes its brainstorming process as "focused chaos." They don't get too attached to their first few design ideas because they know they will change and improve. They may select a couple of alternatives to pursue (out of a half-dozen developed by competing teams) after a charrette, or cherry-pick ideas from multiple sources to create yet another alternative—all to ensure the final design has benefited from a series of explorations and perspectives. In this case, an internal competitive environment can indeed push outcomes to new heights. (See description of IDEO's design of a shopping cart later in this chapter.)

The physical environment of an office can reflect and influence its culture. Ryan asserts something as simple as a big open space—no special offices, no closed doors, and no cubicles—promotes an atmosphere of shared experience, mutual respect, and casual (and nonhierarchical) exchange. For example, an impromptu gathering around someone's computer is common when they have discovered something of architectural interest or "to kick ideas around." EDI, like IDEO, also places a premium on humor and playfulness—whether it's a nickname for a principal or their computers spewing quotes from cartoons when new email is detected—to relieve stress and encourage whacky thinking. IDEO even has a wing of an old DC-3 airliner cantilevered over a meeting room.

As a vital part of its firm culture, which is also under the umbrella of professional development, Torti Gallas, a Silver Spring, Maryland, practice, developed firm committees, firm-wide "discourses," and a customized project management course. Staff at all levels participate on the committees, which primarily address office operations such as marketing and public relations, and document standards. The work of some of the committees is disseminated through a monthly session called a "discourse." The discourse is also a forum for change and evolution in the firm, and helps to build consensus and ownership in shaping new directions. Principal Thomas Gallas[17] says that the firm's design charter, for example, arose from a discussion about improving the quality of architecture and included a set of principles that was signed—and embraced—by everyone in the office. Finally, the Torti Gallas project management course is directed to interns and involves one-on-one training (during personal time) complete with homework and tests, and is a means to "get a common mindset about the importance of project management," according to Thomas Gallas. The firm was recognized by the AIA in 2005 as the IDP Firm of the Year—large firm category for its learning culture and initiatives.

If you're successful, you're in jeopardy of becoming complacent. So get out of your corner office, fail often, argue respectfully with coworkers, adopt a learning culture, don't accept anything at face value, and start to collaborate and innovate.

ADVANCING THE WORK

TEAM COMPOSITION AND SIZE

Getting the right team together is part of the design problem. Team size matters— and typically varies as a function of project scale, complexity, and phase, ramping up from preliminary design to construction documents, becoming smaller during construction. While there is no magic number, in general the larger the team, the more time-intensive and difficult it is to manage communication, relationships, performance, and quality and coordination of the collective work product. Mentoring is certainly more challenging with large teams, claims Roger Goldstein,[18] as "younger staff feel like small cogs in a big machine, dissociated from the essence of the project." His firm mitigates the fragmentary nature of this situation by having each person take responsibility for all consultant coordination related to their domain with oversight by the project manager.

Diversity across the board makes for the best teams. The best teams are composed of highly competent individuals with at least a modicum of interpersonal skills and a balanced mix of personalities, passions, experience, and expertise. At Gensler, team leaders staff their projects with a combination of junior and senior people from multiple disciplines so there is a range of voices around the table. That, together with launching projects in a charrette fashion, amounts to a bit of "design combustion that focuses the team around a shared vision for success and innovation," asserts Jordan Goldstein.[19] After design direction is addressed, frequently there are "breakout sessions by trade to do deep dives into more intricate design issues." Moreover, participation by everyone in the charrette activity itself contributes to motivating the team.

According to recent research reported in the *Harvard Business Review*,[20] a mix of those team members with different cognitive styles such as "creatives," detail-oriented people, and conformists can together promote creativity and innovation. The conformists facilitate cooperation, support the other members, and instill confidence in the work. Creatives may provide the great ideas but are complemented by the detail-oriented types who can ensure that the work gets implemented on time and on budget.

The design team is dynamic; members join and depart at various times as a function of the project circumstance, and expertise and experience of the member. New members can infuse the team with fresh ideas and mitigate the insular thinking that tends to prevail among team members who know each other well. How does the architect optimize the contributions of both part-time and full-time team members?

- **Create a studio (or war room).** Collaborators need a shared place where team members can periodically get together face-to-face and work. A common work area is highly desirable to optimize high-quality interaction among those with diverse personalities, skill sets, and experiences. One caveat: sometimes, serendipitous collaboration can occur while in a coffee shop, at the water cooler, or while waiting for a plane, among other places. Always be open to discussing and advancing the work no matter what the context.

- **Take time.** Time is an essential investment at project inception—and even before an agreement is signed—to optimize both schedule and resources. (1) Clearly define the project and its scope, or at least have all the appropriate questions necessary to define the work, and (2) develop an outline, preliminary design, or master plan of the process by which the project will be designed and delivered. Include all collaborators and their respective roles, when they should optimally be involved, and integration nodes in which individual and multidisciplinary teams should come together.

- **Think like an architect.** The conventional wisdom about integrated project delivery is to *stop* thinking like an architect, i.e., do not emulate the cliché Howard Roark control freak. No, no, no! Rather, keep thinking like an architect—design and maintain control of the process.

- **Start the project with a charrette and include all stakeholders.** (See below for more on charrettes, workshops, and brainstorming sessions.) This will facilitate getting to know the collaborators personally and professionally as well as their ability to work with others on the team. It is an opportunity to observe and assess professional expertise and social skills. Lay out as much information about the project as possible to get the best possible input from all present. Describe the charrette process (visually and verbally) to the team in the first meeting with proposals for specific roles and tasks; project expectations; and leadership, decision-making, and communication protocol.

CHARRETTES, WORKSHOPS, AND BRAINSTORMING SESSIONS

Charrettes, workshops, and brainstorming are among various terms used to describe a collaborative work session in which there is an uninterrupted, total immersion in design investigations in a compressed time frame dedicated to creating the building design—or alternatively the session is highly focused on some aspect of the design. The ideal times to conduct these sessions are at project inception, to jump-start design thinking, and at the various integration nodes (or those points of significant information exchange with consultants) during the course of the project. (See Chapter 4, for elaboration on this topic.) These sessions ensure the active participation of the key consultants and stakeholders, and, at the start, are a means to fully grasp all the programmatic, site, and budget factors; to develop more detailed questions; and to elicit critical feedback on preliminary ideas and the overarching vision for the project.

Brainstorming—the creative collaborative process used across many professions, industries, and businesses—has been successfully deployed in some form for many years. First described by Alex Osborn[21] in 1939, many of the principles outlined below are still valid today and are amenable to collaboration in architectural design. They are worth repeating and underscoring.

- **_Do not criticize or judge ideas._** Evaluation should occur _after_ the collaborative session—not while brainstorming is in process, otherwise (1) team members will be reticent about speaking up and (2) kernels of potentially novel ideas will not have a chance for discussion and development. Work hard to mitigate the natural tendency that we all have to constantly evaluate.

- **_Generate unfettered, wild, and crazy ideas._** In addition to generating the usual array of standard or expected solutions, this strategy has a greater probability of leading to a solution that is innovative and creative.

- **_Try to develop as many ideas as possible._** The more ideas that are on the table—flawed or not—the better chance to trigger something special and excellent. Perfection is not the goal; sheer quantity is.

- **_Combine and build upon ideas._** Synthesizing or improving upon ideas that have been proposed should be part of the natural progression of a brainstorming session. This is one of the unique and wonderful outcomes of collaborative work.

Several additional salient observations with regard to leading brainstorming sessions include the following. It almost goes without saying that the leader should not be condescending, arrogant, or egotistical because the quieter members will be even more reluctant to participate. At regular intervals, or after the session, take stock and summarize important points, design ideas, features, etc. and compare those to the overarching objectives for the project. The leader can be the facilitator for the session but also the designer of it, ensuring appropriate engagement and accomplishment in accordance with the distinctive role of each collaborator and, of course, the agenda.

Keep the brainstorming team as small as possible; as a general rule, less than ten is best although sessions can work with many more participants. And, notwithstanding the inherent excitement of such a session in kicking off a project, one secondary benefit is the camaraderie among collaborators in creating something special together. It should be noted that sessions may be more productive if team members prepare before a session—but not too much, so that they are not overly scripted and can be free to wing-it in response to input from other collaborators.

Figures 3.2–3 Examples of quintessential brainstorming sessions. These photographs capture the energy, excitement, and dynamic engagement inherent in a successful collaborative effort. (Images courtesy of IDEO.)

An outstanding example of brainstorming was documented by ABC News *Nightline* anchor Ted Koppel and correspondent Jack Smith,[22] who visited the design and innovation firm IDEO in Palo Alto in 1999. IDEO was asked by ABC to redesign a shopping cart in just five days to demonstrate what IDEO termed a "deep dive"—a form of design collaboration involving "a process of enlightened trial and error."

There was no hierarchy among team members—no titles and no assigned positions except for the leader. (The project leader was selected because of his ability with groups not because of seniority.) The team was described as "eclectic and diverse." Initially, the team split into smaller groups to conduct interviews and a bit of research to find out what the people who use, make, and repair shopping carts think. These people were viewed as experts who could enable the entire team to learn as much as possible about the issues as quickly as possible. They also wanted to ensure that all stakeholders' points of view were represented. The smaller groups reconvened to share everything they learned.

On the next day, brainstorming began. Ideas in the form of quick sketches and notes written on Post-its were placed on the walls. The team narrowed down the hundreds of ideas by voting. Criteria for selection: an idea must be both "cool and able to be built in a day." Time constraints moved the leader to become autocratic and suggest (1) ending the brainstorming process and (2) deciding "what things will be worked on."

Teams were subdivided to focus on one of the following areas: shopping, safety, checkout, and finding what you're looking for in the store. Each team built a prototype reflecting their area of focus. Then the final step. There was a coalescing of design ideas; the best elements from each prototype were combined into a new, completely redesigned shopping cart.

IDEO has mantras posted on the walls of their studio. They are worth sharing because they are basically an update of Osborn's four principles (previously noted) with the addition of these: (1) one conversation at a time, and (2) stay focused.

OVERVIEW OF TRADITIONAL COLLABORATIVE PRECEDENTS

There is really nothing new about architects, clients, and consultants collaborating. William Caudill, FAIA, of the firm Caudill Rowlett Scott, coined the term *squatters* in the 1950s to describe meetings between the architect, engineering consultants, owner, and building users—on the owner's home turf before design began—to program, clarify values, and brainstorm ideas. What is new, however, is a renewed interest in collaboration due to the promulgation and increasingly broad acceptance of integrated project delivery (IPD) and building information modeling (BIM). See

Chapter 4, Collaboration and technology, for a detailed discussion on IPD and BIM. Also new is a greater appreciation of the benefits of collaborating.

The late Joseph Esherick of the firm Esherick, Homsey, Dodge and Davis certainly understood a fundamental value of collaborating. He encouraged architects to talk to just about everyone involved in the construction of a building including subcontractors—the electricians, plumbers, carpenters, and so on—to inform design decisions and to help solve problems.

THE FILM INDUSTRY AND ARCHITECTURE

There may be a strong analogy between making movies and making buildings. Collaborative effort is necessary to the success of each endeavor. The idea of assembling a team of experts by forming ad hoc alliances appropriate for a specific project (be it a movie or a building)—whether considered networked, virtual, or merely an assemblage of talent in a discrete entity—can be a powerful strategy to deliver a project. Only the best people work on the project, which the architect—or director—selects and leads.

In film, as in architecture, there are schedule and budget constraints in addition to the challenge of managing talent. Extending the analogy, a film's technical crews, i.e., sound, costumes, and lighting, have their own crews, similar to engineering consultants who have their own staff. People who frequently don't know each other often have to become immediate coworkers—and collaborators.

One of the greatest directors of all time, Ingmar Bergman, represents the essence of a collaborative approach in film-making. He wrote the script—sometimes outlined only with ideas—and planned the production process, which served as the creative foundation for the subsequent collaboration with the actors in production. An article in the *Harvard Business Review*[23] explains Bergman's objective: "Bergman wants to capture the fresh, creative urge that occurs in acting of the highest caliber, which is characterized by a spontaneity that cannot be practiced in advance"—or independently. So, Bergman sets forth the concept and vision for the film and enables the other team members to build on his ideas and make them better or use them as a point of departure. This could just as well be a description of an ideal collaborative approach to designing a building.

Director Arthur Penn is profiled in the same article.[24] Similar to Bergman, his collaboration with actors was paramount. "He needed them to behave in ways that were spontaneous, authentic, original, and imaginative; to take risks by trying things they perhaps had never tried before; to be open to his suggestions and ideas; and to develop new ideas of their own and work with them. He was constantly open to the moment, not only abandoning his own preconceived ideas about how a line or scene should be played, but also actively helping actors shed their own preconceptions as well." In this way, Penn was able to promote innovation and create a work of art.

The final point with regard to a director's approach to collaboration is in his or her relationship to the technical crews such as sound and lighting. There are some directors who choose to delegate oversight in this realm to heads of the respective crews. The architectural analogy is to delegate responsibility to consulting engineers who lead their respective teams in their own deep dives.

CREW RESOURCE MANAGEMENT

Crew resource management (CRM) evolved from a workshop sponsored by the National Aeronautics and Space Administration in 1979. The workshop focused on human error in air crashes, and the research concluded that most of the failures were in the realms of interpersonal communications, leadership, and decision-making—in other words, the crew's inability to collaborate effectively. The notion of CRM training was subsequently developed to improve flight crew performance, and is defined as the effective utilization of all available resources—equipment and people—to achieve

Figure 3.4   Crew resource management (CRM), widely embraced by the aviation industry, is relevant to collaboration in architecture. If one member of a team sees a clear advantage in a position or course of action, then it is incumbent on that individual to advance that option persuasively. Pictured here is the cockpit crew for the no. 2 A380's first flight. (© Airbus SAS 2013, photo by P. Masclet.)

safe, efficient flight operations. The overarching objective of CRM is successful teamwork as a function of both technical proficiency and interpersonal dynamics. CRM training has been embraced by the aviation industry worldwide, and has been adapted to other settings as well including fire services, healthcare (operating and emergency rooms), and industries such as nuclear power plants and offshore oil operations.

So what are the basic elements of CRM[25] that are relevant to collaboration in architecture? Assertiveness and advocacy are important behaviors. The key take-home message from CRM is for collaborators to advocate clearly and assertively—yet respectfully—for suggestions, ideas, concerns, and a course of action. It is important to speak up for a position, especially if you feel passionately about it, or disagree with someone else's position. Be willing to ask probing questions about a course of action, for example, and express opinions forcefully and gracefully (i.e., without being threatening) if necessary for the good of the project. As a final step, ensure that everyone understands the perspective and is on board.

When ideas, schemes, or proposals are being evaluated, team members are sometimes reluctant to call attention to a frankly bad idea because they don't want to embarrass or undermine another team member, or because the team member may be too intimidating. Notwithstanding previously described strategies for constructive criticism and communication, the message must be conveyed. As part of the culture of collaboration, there should be a tacit understanding among all collaborators that assertive inquiry is an important part of the process, and ostensibly benefits the work.

The essence of CRM, then, interpreted for collaboration in architecture, is that if one member of a team sees a clear advantage in an alternative or different course of action, then it is incumbent on that individual to advance that option persuasively. Elite teams and great leaders have been practicing this well before the promulgation of CRM; sometimes it is valuable to recall strategies that have made great teams great.

LEARNING FROM THE ORCHESTRA

If architecture, according to Goethe, is frozen music, then collaboration is an orchestra playing a symphony. To orchestrate is to collaborate to maximum effect. The orchestra demonstrates—perhaps more than anything else—the benefit of strong and responsive leadership; leadership by enthusiasm, energy, and feeling as opposed to leadership by criticism or narcissism. What follows are some observations about an orchestra that may provide some insights into successful collaboration in architecture.

- **Don't underestimate the importance of the leader.** The conductor is the *single individual* who "establishes and maintains the rhythm, drives the emphasis, and

Figure 3.5   James Gaffigan leading the Juilliard Orchestra in Mahler's Symphony no. 4 at Alice Tully Hall on April 20, 2013. If architecture, according to Goethe, is frozen music, then collaboration is an orchestra playing a symphony. (Photo by Hiroyuki Ito/Getty Images.)

controls the tone of the piece being played."[26] The architect, likewise, is the one who creates the concept and vision for a project, designs and directs the process, sets the ground rules, and inspires the collaborators. And collaborators must be mindful of and appreciate different leadership styles.

■ *The best people play with passion and great skill.* Musicians—or architects and their consultants—must be selected with that in mind as a prerequisite to joining the team and creating a work of art.

■ *Musicians understand their relationships to the whole yet are highly individualistic.* Individuality should be cultivated. Working well in a collaborative environment toward shared objectives and preserving individuality are not mutually exclusive. Awareness of what other sections/consultants are doing is part of the process.

■ *Musicians have impeccable timing.* Knowing when to participate and to what extent is particularly salient for collaborators (or for directing the collaborators).

■ *The conductor is the only one who sees the big picture.* Architects, as well, are in this unique position; this is one reason why collaboration should not be a democracy.

- ▣ *The conductor knows the musicians.* The conductor knows their strengths and limitations, and knows how to get the best effort from them. Architects need to be cognizant of their collaborators' unique abilities and must ensure that there is appropriate and ongoing critique and reciprocal communication to elicit innovative work.

- ▣ *Fresh interpretations of the music are inspiring.* So too is looking at standard building types in innovative ways.

COLLABORATIVE TEAM AS A FAMILY

In sum, a traditional collaborative partnership is one that is usually characterized by mutual obligations and personal relationships with an unselfish flavor. The original Mafia doctrine, "Friends of friends," describes a network of individuals bound by mutual obligations, openness and transparency, mutual benefit, shared risks and rewards, and accountability, i.e., family.

NOTES

1. Claire Cain Miller and Catherine Rampell, "Yahoo Orders Home Workers Back to the Office," *The New York Times*, February 25, 2013.

2. Henry Fonda (Producer), Sidney Lumet (Director), *12 Angry Men* (motion picture). United States of America: Orion-Nova Productions, 1957.

3. Rob Sheehan, personal communication with the author, June 29, 2007.

4. William Rawn, FAIA, personal communication with the author, June 20, 2007.

5. Sarah Harkness, quoted by the author in *Curing the Fountainheadache: How Architects and their Clients Communicate*, 2e, New York: Sterling Publishing Co., 2006, p. 59.

6. Morris A. Nunes, personal communication with the author, October 29, 2008.

7. Jordan Goldstein, personal communication with the author, November 4, 2008.

8. Morris A. Nunes, personal communication with the author, October 29, 2008.

9. Bill Parcells, quoted in *The New York Times Sports Magazine*, November 2006, p. 51.

10. *NAAB Conditions for Accreditation*, "3.5 Studio Culture," Washington, DC: National Architectural Accrediting Board, 2004.

11. Jean R. Valence, *Architect's Essentials of Professional Development*, Hoboken, NJ: John Wiley & Sons, 2003, p. 13.

12. Robert I. Sutton, *Weird Ideas that Work: How to Build a Creative Company*, New York: Free Press, 2002.

13. Olson Kundig Architects, "Firm Culture," www.olsonkundigarchitects.com/About/FirmCulture (accessed April 30, 2013).

14. Roger Goldstein, personal communication with the author, November 3, 2008.

15. Michael Ryan, personal communication with the author, October 12, 2007.

16. ABC News, *Nightline*, "The Deep Dive: One Company's Secret Weapon for Innovation," July 13, 1999.

17. Thomas Gallas, personal communication with the author, October 25, 2007.

18. Roger Goldstein, personal communication with the author, November 3, 2008.

19. Jordan Goldstein, personal communication with the author, November 4, 2008.

20. Ella Miron-Spektor, Miriam Erez, and Eitan Naveh, "Teamwork: To Drive Creativity Add Some Conformity," *Harvard Business Review*, vol. 90 no. 3, March 2012, p. 30.

21. Alex F. Osborn, *Applied Imagination: Principles and Procedures of Creative Thinking*, Iyer Press reprint 2011 (first printing 1953), pp. 297–301.

22. ABC News, *Nightline*, "The Deep Dive: One Company's Secret Weapon for Innovation," July 13, 1999.

23. Eileen Morley and Andrew Silver, "A Film Director's Approach to Managing Creativity," *Harvard Business Review*, vol. 55 no. 2, March–April 1977, p. 64.

24. Eileen Morley and Andrew Silver, "A Film Director's Approach to Managing Creativity," *Harvard Business Review*, vol. 55 no. 2, March–April 1977, p. 66.

25. James E. Driskell and Richard J. Adams, *Crew Resource Management: An Introductory Handbook*, Washington, DC: U.S. Department of Transportation Federal Aviation Administration, 1992, pp. 8–32.

26. "Ten Things Entrepreneurs Can Learn from Musicians," http://blog.crowdspring.com/2011/03/10-things-that-entrepreneurs-can-learn-from-musicians/ (accessed April 18, 2013).

A logical next chapter in this book about relationships and collaboration in architecture should include a discussion related to the most recent advances in technology and project delivery. I have intentionally not discussed building information modeling (BIM) and integrated project delivery (IPD) in previous chapters because collaboration skills and processes transcend technology and tools, and should be considered independently. Software by itself does not cultivate meaningful engagement.

This is an incredibly exciting time to practice architecture. The challenge of creating excellent designs, even magical buildings that inspire, which has always been present, is now part of an even bigger, evolving challenge to discover new practice opportunities (given the volatile economic climate) and better ways to deliver projects. Innovative practice is now part of the mix with innovative design. Therefore, service delivery—the

4

COLLABORATION AND TECHNOLOGY

organizational and operational modes of practice—should be flexible as a function of unique project and market circumstances.

Certainly BIM and IPD present one excellent project delivery strategy that requires collaborative effort for translating ideas into buildings. However, to be optimally responsive, and to provide the best professional service to our clients, a range of traditional and nontraditional contracting arrangements must be considered. BIM/IPD will be with us now and in the conceivable future, but so will other modes of project delivery. The choice is not, and will not always be, straightforward or a foregone conclusion.

BUILDING INFORMATION MODELING AND INTEGRATED PROJECT DELIVERY

There are many definitions of BIM appearing in literature from software vendors, professional and industry organizations, and various books and publications, primarily because it is constantly developing. Common to many of those definitions and in general terms, BIM is a process (analogous to IPD—to make things more confusing) and a business model. But fundamentally, it is characterized by the parametric object-based software that is used to create not only a three-dimensional model of a virtual building, but also drawings and rich databases of information that can include such things as budget estimates, construction schedules, quantities takeoffs, and fabrication details. Parametric modeling allows for substantial changes to be made quickly and for easy coordination and clash detection to occur.

A number of features that can be deployed within the BIM environment (among many others) include energy analyses, building lifecycle costs, and code compliance checks in schematic design, and facilities management (operations and maintenance) post-construction. Use of BIM in facilities management is very appealing to an increasing number of owners. Clearly, there can be huge benefits to collaborative processes within a BIM environment.

Software that incorporates building information modeling capabilities is primarily responsible for enabling—some say forcing—integrated project delivery. IPD, simply stated, is the project delivery method defined by collaboration among all stakeholders with a sharing of information, risk, and reward.

DESIGN THINKING

The discussion of the art of collaboration in architecture would not be complete without maintaining a sharp focus on our collective goal of creating magical, delightful, and wonderful places to live, work, and play. Developing initial design concepts for those environments is sometimes very personal and idiosyncratic. Tools such as napkins, sketchbooks, and thick markers, as well as the ability to deftly move in and out of different software—and between tools and media—will always have a place in a collaborative design process.

It is critical to make a distinction between design thinking and design software. Design software is certainly very well suited to production (design development and construction document phases) in which there are many redundant tasks as well as requirements to manipulate and share information. And earlier in the design process, in schematic design for example, analyses of building models such as energy modeling can be valuable for making quantitatively informed design decisions in climate-dominated, high-performance buildings.

However, and this is an important point to underscore, design imagination and creativity are uniquely human traits. The architect's personality, personal vision, and design agenda are often quite salient in shaping ideas. Ideas—architectural design concepts—can be inspired by many different personal experiences, sources, triggers, project circumstances, critical reflection, and so on. In other words, ideas, innovation, or the magic underlying a concept for a building arises from a certain way of *design* thinking. Design thinking can incorporate associative thinking, thinking out of the box, metaphorical thinking, linking previously unlinked concepts, viewing things in fresh ways, and, especially, collaborative thinking.

Drawing is an integral part of the design process. In 1968, William Kirby Lockard[1] made a plea for "drawing as a means to architecture ... drawing must never become the end." And in 2013, Michael Graves,[2] in response to what he views as a fashionable declaration in many architectural circles that drawing is dead (due to the computer), stated, "Drawings are not just end products: they are part of the thought process of architectural design. Drawings express the interaction of our minds, eyes and hands. This last statement is absolutely crucial to the difference between those who draw to conceptualize architecture and those who use the computer." Even though in different eras, Lockard's and Graves's statements are eerily similar and independent of hardware and software technology.

What does all this have to do with collaboration? Drawing—sketching and diagramming—is the language of building and architecture that communicates design concepts; that reveals opportunities for building upon, triggering, and critiquing ideas; and that enables collaboration among diverse stakeholders. Drawing is a device for creative, action-oriented collaboration and "reflective conversation with the situation [you] are shaping."[3] Freehand drawings represent a snapshot of design thinking (see Figures 4.1 and 4.2).

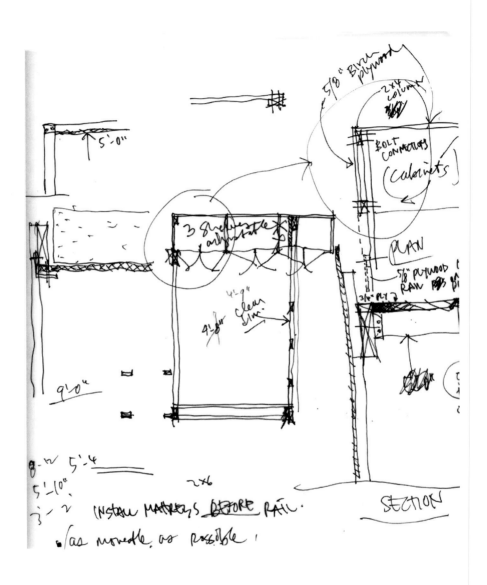

Figures 4.1–2 The hand-drawn sketches capture design thinking in action. Plan, section, and perspective are developed concurrently for a bridge linking platform beds in adjacent rooms for 7-year-old twins.

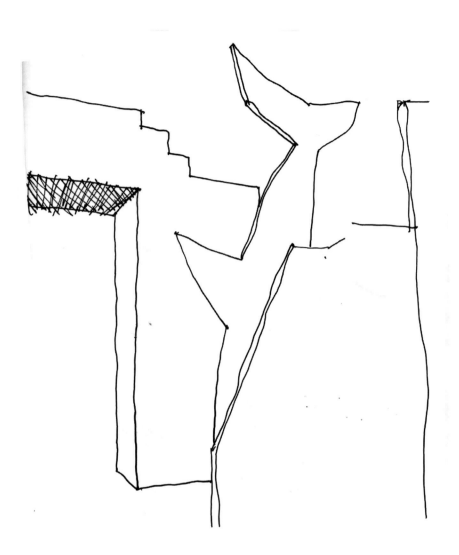

There is a full spectrum of tools to facilitate and record this thinking in the early stages of design. They include drawings, tracing paper, yellow stickies, thick markers, newsprint, whiteboard, three-dimensional modeling design software, and physical models (cardboard, clay, paper), among others. Varying, shifting, and merging tools and media can spark new perspectives. Do not underestimate the power of serendipity and playing; new ideas may emerge just by using a new tool.

A skillful collaborator has at his or her disposal both digital and physical (i.e., freehand drawing) methods, and recognizes that they elicit different dimensions of creativity. Sketching by itself cannot push the design envelope in certain directions as far as evolving software and computing can.

The complete model approach of BIM software is very seductive, but it should be critically evaluated on each project for its exclusive use in the initial stages of the collaborative process. (There are exceptions; see below.) The technology is not an end in itself; it is easy to lose sight of the big picture because of the steep learning curve—the immersion, time, and energy required to learn the software and apply it to design and construction processes. The overarching message is that any process, tool, or vehicle that can be deployed at any stage of a project can and should be deployed if it will enhance the design, performance, or some aspect of a project. This is where getting creative about the process can be meaningful; the following illustrates an example.

One of the liberating ideas of IPD is that there is flexibility in how and when BIM software can be deployed and integrated with other tools and modes of collaboration. Given certain project circumstances, a BIM model may be very valuable in modeling generic shading strategies on building façades at the earliest stages of a project. Once analyzed to reduce energy consumption, the generic design can then be developed with other tools, such as hand sketching, which can then be plugged back into the BIM model. This can become an iterative cycle, with both drawing and design software acting as great collaborative tools. A notable example of this process is the remodeling of the EGWW Federal Building in Portland, Oregon, by SERA Architects and Cutler Anderson Architects. Cutler artfully detailed the façade design using hand sketches and SERA worked them into the BIM model (and vice versa) until an optimal scheme was reached.[4] Transitioning to BIM does not necessarily mean completely abandoning sketching or physical model-making. Optimize the benefits of every tool as a function of the design problem.

There are some individuals who are quite adept and comfortable using BIM software for preliminary design, not just production. One argument in support of this process is that there are huge efficiency gains by avoiding duplication of effort in multiple applications or with use of other tools. Another argument promoting exclusive BIM use on small projects, exemplified by François Lévy,[5] suggests that BIM can be a great design environment and BIM data can inform the design process. Lévy asserts that small buildings are skin-load dominated, and the smaller the building, the greater that climate influences how it uses energy. BIM, with its energy analysis features, can be a great assist in making quantitatively informed design decisions for high-performance buildings in the earliest stages of design.

There are limitations to algorithmic computation, particularly in the early stages of collaborative design. No technology fully encompasses how a designer or collaborative team thinks. With all the significant innovations and possibilities with BIM and other software, there are inherent biases with any modeling tool that make it less convenient to think in other ways. Geoffrey Adams,[6] Associate Professor at the University of New Mexico, elaborates: "The more complicated and layered a software tool is, the more likely it is to privilege certain methods of working." Adams advises that one always be cognizant of both what the tool is doing *to* the design process as well as what it can do *for* it. In other words, use the tool wisely to take advantage of its great benefits in supporting design and making design better, not compromising design for expedience in some other aspect. Employ tools in the beginning stages of a design project that best augment three-dimensional imagination and abstract thinking.

BIM WORKFLOWS AND MANAGED COLLABORATION

Managed collaboration, as described in Chapter 2, is very much in alignment with an effective and efficient BIM workflow. This is particularly applicable from the design development phase to project completion. The individual consultant teams collaborate intensively among themselves, creating their own models with their own specialized software to optimally do their part of the work. The various models come together—they are "amalgamated" or "aggregated" by the architect into an evolving single project model at regular intervals, and at various integration points, which is when the bulk of the collaborative work across disciplines is accomplished. This will become easier as interoperability (data exchange) between various software applications and versions becomes widespread. Obviously, these information exchanges must be planned with all stakeholders from project inception as an integral part of the process to ensure (1) compatibility of files (for example, through an Industry Foundation Classes [IFC] file format) and (2) alignment of expectations for resolution of the work, "level of development," or specific content of each significant submission.

This process should work smoothly because many of the major design decisions have already been made in preliminary design (whether or not BIM software has been used from inception). The architect, as design team leader, ensures that the work across disciplines is resolved and developed appropriately at the integration points, consistent with the overarching project goals, vision, and concepts. During this part of the process, the model is the primary vehicle for the collaborative effort.

WORKSHOP AND CRITICAL REFLECTION AT EACH INTEGRATION NODE

A workshop or mini-charrette is an inspiring way to advance and manage the project at integration nodes (or at those points of significant information exchange). A workshop is deployed at certain times during a project as a means to collaborate more vigorously and deeply. At each workshop, the design becomes more resolved and integrated, problems are addressed, and work is coordinated. The workshop is a vehicle to engage in in-depth discussions with all consultants, the owner, and other stakeholders as appropriate.

Structuring this workshop process for each integration node is, in itself, another design problem for the architect. Collaboration across specialty teams occurs at the integration nodes, which must be specifically defined for the project at hand to best utilize the consultants and tools in the context of the project circumstances.

Only relevant stakeholders should participate as collaborators in these unique, highly focused sessions in which there is an intensive, total immersion in a compressed, uninterrupted, and dedicated time frame focused on a review of work to date, design analysis, and integration at the appropriate level of detail. It not only affirms that the design is progressing in accordance with initial ideas (aesthetic and social purpose, cost issues, sustainability goals, and so on) but provides a roadmap for advancing it to the next increment of resolution and integration. These workshops provide extraordinary opportunities to expose the project to a high-level critical analysis and reflection by all collaborators. "Criticism can make us see familiar things from new perspectives, shake us out of our shopworn habits, and provoke us into thinking about problems we might otherwise overlook."[7]

Insightful criticism can be folded into the design process at each workshop so that projects can become better—and innovative. This is one of the most important aspects of the workshop component of this collaborative process, the BIM workflow, and IPD in general. The workshop held during an integration node is not just about coordination, clash detection, constructability, cost, energy optimization, and all the other myriad features. At the risk of being redundant, it is an opportunity to thoughtfully and collectively consider design: the big picture and vision, and how they are developing for the project. Yes, the workshop can be used to reap all the benefits of BIM, but this is to implore you to do more: exploit the efficiencies of the process by directing more high-quality designer time to create a meaningful, significant work of architecture.

The architect provides guidance for next steps, including responses to the critical assessments and experimenting or innovating to advance the design scheme (which may also serve to inspire the team). After processing the architect's vision, concept, early design ideas, and subsequent direction after every workshop, the consultants should be free to infuse their work with their own interpretation of that information and guidance. The architect's leadership should ensure that this happens, so that the consultants are truly invested in the project. Moreover, a workshop also has a benefit of mitigating against feelings of isolation by team members, and promoting feelings of investment in the project and contributing to design decisions.

After a couple of these workshops have been completed—once there has been some success in designing together—a social gathering might be propitious. It can serve to nurture relationships and set the tone for energetically completing the project.

In sum, the workshop deployed at integration nodes is an exciting, inspiring, and effective brainstorming strategy to identify key issues, resolve problems, critically reflect on the design, and advance the project. The architect designs each workshop with a focus on some aspect of the design to elicit high-quality and immediate feedback on which to base further design investigation and inquiry.

LINKING DESIGN THINKING AND COLLABORATION

BIM software is a tool that should be used in support of your particular collaborative design process—not to dictate it (i.e., the tail should not wag the dog!). And managed collaboration can give you a handle on defining that process. As previously noted, there are many different tools and unique approaches to arriving at a schematic design. The workflow in the early design phase can be idiosyncratic, and not necessarily amenable to BIM use. But designs can certainly be imported into the BIM environment after, or concurrently with, schematics to take advantage of its many benefits. As with any great tool, BIM can be used and leveraged as a function of your comfort and facility with it. In sum, don't lose sight of our reason for being architects, which of course is to do great design. Software—or any tool—must reinforce that, first and foremost.

Virtual practice, managed collaboration, and BIM: what could be better for engaging select projects at any scale now and in the future? Flexibility is one key to creating ad hoc alliances composed of experts and specialists who are assembled on the fly for each unique project (and then are disbanded when the project ends). Termed "teaming," it is analogous to "a pickup basketball game rather than plays run by a team that has trained as a unit," or "clinicians in an emergency room who convene quickly to solve a specific patient problem" rather than a surgical team that has performed the same procedure many times.[8] In architecture, a computer with a lot of memory, a high-speed Internet connection, and a network of *skilled* collaborators will set you in the right direction to be optimally responsive to just about any opportunity and challenge. Augment that with the occasional face-to-face meeting or workshop and the infrastructure for managed collaboration will be established.

It behooves all of us as architects to apply as much design thinking to shape a new collaborative model of practice—on each unique project—as we do to creating buildings. It is the thoughtful assimilation of this collaborative model (including the most appropriate tools and technology) in support of design excellence and a true service ethic that will define the best in professional practice. However, with all the emphasis on collaborative processes of one form or another, it is important to keep in mind that process must always lead to tangible outcomes. These include a successful building (however that may be defined), a satisfied client, and sufficient profit in support of a thriving firm.

NOTES

1. William Kirby Lockard, *Drawing as a Means to Architecture*, New York: Van Nostrand Reinhold Company, 1968, p. 5.

2. Michael Graves, "Architecture and the Lost Art of Drawing," *The New York Times*, September 1, 2012.

3. Donald A. Schön, *The Reflective Practitioner: How Professionals Think in Action*, New York: Basic Books, Inc., 1983, p. 103.

4. Nalina Moses, "SERA's Portland Federal Building: Big Data, Big Buildings, Big BIM," *AIA Architect*, The American Institute of Architects, www.aia.org/practicing/AIAB097962 (accessed March 8, 2013).

5. François Lévy, presenter at Nemetschek Vectorworks BIM Camp, District Architecture Center, Washington, DC, January 24, 2013.

6. Geoffrey Adams quoted by the author in "Integrated Practice in Perspective: A New Model for the Architectural Profession," *Architectural Record*, vol. 195 no. 5, May 2007, p. 120.

7. Christopher Mead, "Critical Thinking in Architectural Design," *Architectural Design Portable Handbook*, New York: McGraw-Hill, 2001, pp. 42–43.

8. Amy C. Edmondson, "Teamwork on the Fly," *Harvard Business Review*, vol. 90 no. 4, April 2012, p. 74.

In an effort to present a balanced picture of the benefits and challenges of collaborative efforts on complex architectural projects, the following snapshots illustrate examples of successful and unsuccessful aspects of collaboration. Critical reflection on that work is valuable in crystallizing the lessons for readers. It is also a model of the importance of reflective practice as a final step and integral component of any collaborative undertaking, regardless of style or approach. Almost by definition, the snapshots and case study presented demonstrate what I've referred to as a traditional approach to collaboration. As you read and think about them, consider how a "managed" or "integrated" style of practice might influence the trajectory and outcomes of each situation.

To emphasize the relevance of collaboration across associated disciplines and from multiple perspectives, the essays and case study in this chapter are written by educators and a constructor as well as architects.

SNAPSHOTS OF EFFECTIVE AND INEFFECTIVE COLLABORATION

TEAM FAILURES

In his essay below, Mark C. Childs demonstrates the value of investing time to critically reflect on process. Childs is a Professor of Architecture at the University of New Mexico. His most recent book is *Urban Composition: Developing Community through Design* (Princeton Architectural Press, 2012).

Why would anyone accept Andy Pressman's invitation to write about their failures? It is difficult to think about setbacks, much less write about them in public so that all can second-guess my mistakes. Acknowledging and reflecting upon mistakes, however, is critical for learning. Two types of team failures stand out in my experience, as follows.

1. TEAM COMPOSITION AND MONOCULTURES

When one person starts dancing and inspires 20 others to follow, each person does their dance and the result is a dance party. If these same people tried to bake a single pie by all doing the same thing, there would be a significant amount of wasted effort. Many tasks do not lend themselves to all members of the team engaging in the same activity.

In my early years as a faculty member, I, like many of my colleagues, assembled student teams but failed to fit the team roles and composition to the characteristics of the task. We often had multiple designers trying to bake the same pie. For teams, it is essential that the work of each member adds to the work of others instead of vying for primacy.

My first restructuring was to make "dances" in which everyone could do their own thing in the same place. That is, I assigned each architecture student a different building along a street or in a district so that collectively the separate projects added up to a study of the district. This significantly increased the number of teams that succeeded in producing more than they would have as individuals, and reduced complaints. However, this parallel play did not yet amount to true teamwork.

Next, we added multiple disciplines. Teams whose members have different scopes of responsibility, skills, and goals allow for a separation of tasks. However, a new set of problems arise when one moves from a monocultural team to a team ecosystem. Divergent goals and standards, for example, can cause team members to believe that the others are unfocused, lazy, or just difficult. Multiple times, I've had architecture students complain that the planning students are just talking, while the planning students believe the architects are just drawing without knowing what the clients and neighbors want. This is often a battle about the order in which steps of a process must take place—neighborhood consultation or exploration of structural possibilities first?

Frequently enough, the steps can come in parallel or any other order and, in most cases, are revisited and revised through multiple iterations. Students typically don't have the experience to know this, and thus we have introduced a set of quick warm-up exercises to uncover and discuss the multiple problems of "tuning" a team ecosystem, such as having students take on each other's role.

Along the way, I also began to challenge and disaggregate the definition of failure. Working in teams is a learned skill. We must allow teams to "fail" early and often and be guided to reflect on what worked, what did not, and why. This requires that we (a) focus on student learning as the primary "product" of a studio, (b) set up a series of exercises that ideally build to a successful team, and (c) create procedures for carrying on after a team "fails," such as establishing from the beginning how each member can produce independent work.

Each member of a team should have a distinct scope of work. Match the composition of roles to the nature of the work, and build in time so that members can understand each other's goals, standards, and ways of working. If the exercise is primarily educational, then allow for failure and reflection.

2. DROPPING THE BATON

In his TED talk Derek Sivers[1] says, "It's important to nurture your first few followers as equals"; those first followers are not only "what transforms a lone nut into a leader," but those who join later follow the first followers. This is a task in which I have repeatedly failed.

Two difficulties I have faced are (a) often respect for the initiator is what draws the initial followers, and (b) the work of organizing and sustaining the group may be easier for the initiator than the first followers. For example, I organized an informal off-campus reading group for interested former students. My idea was to start a group of emerging professionals that would not be dominated by the "old guard," thus I would need to remove myself as soon as possible. Each of three times I (re)started the group, it ran well for a time with initial members taking on organizing roles. Then, when I withdrew, the meeting soon stopped.

There were at least three impediments to nurturing the initial members as equals. First, the history of our relationship as teacher and students provided the basis of trust that the endeavor might be worthwhile. Second, I had an advantage as I knew the current literature that might be of interest, and could readily call on colleagues for various favors to support the group. I had anticipated both of these impediments and actively worked to overcome them by removing the group from the context of school, actively training members in finding appropriate literature, handing off organizational tasks, and setting up the expectation that they would assume leadership of the group. The third impediment, I realized only in sitting down to write this piece, was that even though I enjoyed and benefited from the discussions, I intended that they continue the group and that I leave. At a fundamental level I did not consider myself an equal part of the group. I thought I had the special privilege of leaving without affecting the group, but instead, I set precedent in leaving as I had in starting the group.

This last is not insurmountable (I have succeeded in other cases). Perhaps, if I had been an advisor from the beginning supporting a student convener, then my different role would not prove an impediment. However, the fact that I did not recognize it as an issue from the beginning made it intractable. Often it is these unrecognized impediments and assumptions that generate the most difficult difficulties. That is where reflection upon "failures" is critical—to see what was not visible at the time.

RESEARCH AS A COLLABORATIVE TOOL

Research is increasingly becoming a mainstay of professional practice in architecture. David Riz, AIA, Principal, KieranTimberlake, discusses how research is not only essential to his firm's design process but serves as a means of effectively engaging clients. Riz has 23 years of experience as an architect, and has dedicated much of his practice to developing effective collaboration processes leading to award-winning, sustainably designed buildings.

How can architects create a process that is collaborative, efficient, and empowering? Research is integral to our process of working with owners to arrive at meaningful architecture that is based on a balance of hard facts and intuition. Our designs are heavily data-driven, which helps us remain objective and, in turn, helps clients make sound decisions for the project. We spend significant effort gathering data and establishing goals and metrics, making for a much less contentious discussion with clients, because facts form the basis for opinions. For example, a potential conflict was turned into an asset in developing a storm water strategy for a new building. The client wanted to add an irrigation-dependent landscape to the project, which we initially opposed for sustainability reasons. Even after demonstrating how much water the landscape they wanted would consume annually, it was clear they would not change their minds, so we suggested using the building itself to collect 50 percent of the water needed for irrigation by transporting storm water overflow from the roof and through a sculptural water feature. Storm water management becomes an architecturally evocative way for the client to express its mission visually.

We try to remain impartial at the start of a project, and even after formal issues begin to emerge, we continue to keep objective issues in the foreground. We have seen that when clients understand the science behind a design, they come to appreciate it more because they have a full grasp of its function and logic. And, in times of debate with design review committees or boards, we have seen our clients become great advocates for our design because they feel quite invested in the process that brought them to that point. For example, in a project that we felt needed more transparency for reasons of program and light, the client was concerned that exceeding 40 percent glazing would not meet their stringent energy standards. We developed a series of virtual daylight studies that proved the energy standards could be achieved, with graphics describing the architectural approach, but they were not convinced. To make the point stronger, we fabricated a number of full-scale prototypes in our own shop that demonstrated passive envelope strategies, employing both perforated brick screens and translucent panels. After the client group was sold, the members went on to convince their board to approve the strategy, a victory made even greater because it employed innovative materials not commonly accepted by the client in the past.

No matter how excellent a design idea is, a flawed delivery process inevitably compromises its potential for performance, craftsmanship, and even its basic design intent. This is seen far too often, particularly on projects with public funding, where design–bid–build is gospel, if not law. This is a delivery method based on the premise that conflict, rather than collaboration (or *collusion* as some clients would have it), results in more competition and, therefore, lower first costs. In this arrangement, architect and builder have separate contracts in which clients dictate their respective roles, but the owner's responsibilities in the delivery process are not often codified, leaving it to the architects to search for the right level of engagement. Compounding this is the quickening pace of project development, owing to advances in technology and client-driven desires for shorter schedules; it becomes even more important that all involved parties keep up.

Without processes to develop initial buy-in, or to ensure consistent participation of all parties, frequent opportunities lurk for mischief, beginning in the design phase with scope and cost creep, and ultimately lead to the dreaded value engineering after each phase. As a result, human relationships become adversarial. After months of seemingly running in place, making costly revisions due to late-breaking information, and reconciling budgets gone over, a pall hangs over the project and those working to bring the design to life. This continues through construction when the low bid contractor must be newly initiated into the group. Time is not spent advancing the design, but rather leveraging one's own position, placing enormous financial and mental burden on the collective energy of all involved.

How can we stop this? Architects realize numerous buildings in their lifetimes, gaining expertise on process improvements with each new project, yet this acquired knowledge has little to no influence on how contracts are written by a new client. In a design–bid–build contract, often the working relationship is defined not by an expert in design processes, but by an attorney, whose job is to reduce risk.

Integrated project delivery (IPD) offers some solace, as it is not defined by unseen attorneys, but by people whose expertise is designing and building. With its primary goals to increase value to the owner, reduce waste, and maximize efficiency, it promotes greater collaboration and ideally lessens discord. To deliver a project in an integrated manner, all parties must be in alignment regarding the project values before the design begins. Those values are shared over the course of the project, which facilitates setting goals and metrics for success.

Even before the emergence of IPD, our firm has believed in collective intelligence, and generally employs its principles to all projects—goal setting, values alignment, dynamic cost modeling—regardless of what is defined in a contract. When clients choose IPD we are delighted because usually it means they want to be fully engaged. They are not interested in hierarchy; they are looking for transparency, multiple points of view, and full collaboration.

One example of this is our work on a headquarters for the Energy Efficient Buildings (EEB) Hub, one of three innovation clusters created by the Department of Energy in 2011. A renovation of a World War II-era building, the project will be a living laboratory for commercial buildings, adaptive reuse, and energy efficiency innovation. The design of the delivery process is nearly as precious to the client as the built work, because a big part of the EEB Hub's mission is to provide a roadmap for more efficient project delivery.

The project is guided by an Integrated Design Group, made up of representatives of the architect, builder, and owner, tasked with tactical aspects of shepherding the design. A second group, the Building Steering Committee, made up of client, user, architect, and builder representatives, is responsible for strategic oversight of the project as a whole. These groups meet frequently, and some people are members of both groups to ensure continuity of objectives. Meetings do not end when the design is complete—they continue well into construction. When conflicts or cost issues arise, they are evaluated by the Building Steering Committee, and the Integrated Design Group lives with their conclusions. It is refreshing as an architect to be a member of the committee that makes the final decisions, rather than merely the recipient of those decisions. It allows architects to think about the project in much broader terms than just design, and lets clients understand that they have a responsibility in factors that drive cost. We have never gone "backwards" on this project—all decisions have been made through the filter of the project values.

IPD may not be right for all projects, but it has a lot to offer. For the EEB Hub, it provided a structure for group interactions so that participants could bring the full breadth of their experience to bear in a collaborative way. Because values are aligned early and remain touchstones throughout, future discord is eliminated, not simply because they are words to live by, *but because the collective act of putting them together cannot be underestimated as a way of cementing the team.* It recognizes that, as in a relay race, there are multiple leaders, at different times, with different points of view, and all are integral to the effort. Perhaps most important is that by taking away unreasonable liability, the client frees team members to wade into other areas of expertise, allowing architects to engage critical topics, like the influence of construction logistics in deriving design solutions.

At the end of the day, it comes down to establishing trust. The IPD process *codifies* trust, but it does not *create* trust. We engender trust by making our working processes transparent at the interview stage and throughout the development of a project, and most importantly by listening and responding to client concerns. This works independently of what roles are defined in the contract. We don't do much differently on IPD projects than on any other project. What IPD does is define rules for when decisions are made, and who must be at the table to make them. Our process has an ethic. IPD is a procedure. How do you marry the two?

STRATEGIES FOR DESIGN EXCELLENCE ON LARGE PROJECTS

Roger Schwabacher, AIA, is a Senior Associate and Project Architect with HOK in Washington, DC. In his essay below, Schwabacher discusses large-scale collaborative projects, but the underlying ideas are so universal that the strategies can apply equally to projects of just about any scale. His projects include the King Abdullah Petroleum Studies and Research Center (KAPSARC), a 220-building campus in Riyadh, Saudi Arabia; the LEED[2] Gold certified National Oceanic and Atmospheric Administration (NOAA) Center for Weather and Climate Prediction in College Park, Maryland, USA; and a new office building to double the size of the US Embassy in Moscow, Russia.

The first thing to understand about the process of collaboration on large, complicated projects at HOK is that the design teams have become huge. Team leaders need to inspire not only the creativity of a group of architects, but also to harness diverse opinions from a broad spectrum of individuals such as the landscape architect; interior, sustainable, lighting, and graphic designers; specification writer; structural, mechanical, electrical, plumbing, civil, geotechnical, blast, and fire protection engineers; curtain wall, thermal, maintenance, acoustic, IT, life safety, elevator, hardware, and security consultants; cost estimator; and commissioning agent, not to mention the oftentimes large and diverse client teams. The key to collaborating with such a large group is to empower the group's leader, often the project designer or architect, to solicit opinions from this wide net and to choose the solutions that work best with the overarching design goals of the project. Without this strong leader, who can resolutely make decisions in the best interest of the project, the diversity of opinions will dilute the original design intent.

How then is this strong project leader fostering collaboration and not becoming a dictator? By empowering each individual on the team, giving them a clear understanding of project goals, and providing timely dissemination of information from meetings and discussions.

It has been my experience that different strategies are needed to foster collaboration with what I have identified as three distinct groups: the client, the architectural design team, and the engineers and consultants.

CLIENT

Collaboration sessions with the client, whether in face-to-face meetings, through WebEx, or through an exchange of sketches, need to start with a clear understanding of their organization and how they work. A first, basic step is to make sure that the key decision-makers are involved in the discussions; often this requires wading through layers in the organization to get to the people who have the power to make decisions. Without identifying and including the key decision-makers in these meetings, design efforts can spiral without progress. Once the correct people are identified, a strategy to foster collaboration is to approach the design problems with the client's priorities in mind, which often are very different than the design team's point of view. By "speaking their language" and understanding their key points, the design solution becomes more layered and complex. Listening is a skill often overlooked; collaboration with this group frequently involves helping them to clearly articulate their ideas and translate them into the built form. Tools most often used include three-dimensional renderings, animations, physical samples, project tours, and key facts/numbers about the building—items accessible to people not directly involved in the design and construction industry. Skills needed include *patience* to deal with language barriers and any inexperience with design and construction, *understanding* of cultural differences, and *flexibility* to respond to issues as they arise. The end goal is to gain the client's trust; collaboration does not work if the client is suspicious of your motives or goals.

ARCHITECTURAL DESIGN TEAM

The key to fostering collaboration within a design team is channeling the variety of strong design opinions into a unified goal. On large HOK projects, this team may include up to 20 design professionals including architects, interior designers, landscape architects, sustainable designers, graphic designers, lighting designers, and specification writers. Each of these team members needs to be vested in the project; they are not working on someone else's design, but are creating new ideas and actively developing the design to make the overall project a success. The idea of a "master architect" who makes every decision does not exist in today's practice. With the invention of BIM and the trend towards increasingly complex buildings with greater levels of coordination between disciplines, delegation of responsibility and collaboration between team members is the only way to work with any efficiency.

I have found that design team collaboration works when the overall design intent is clear and designers feel free to add to the vision. It fails when information is guarded, and independent thought is not encouraged. Design leaders need to be open to discussion, available to the team, and have clarity of thought and enthusiasm for the project. Collaboration between peers is also based on trust and respect; while visions may be different, the overall goal of improving the work of the office must be shared.

The best innovations on a project, whether they are overarching themes or specific details, usually come about organically in the design process and most typically occur in group conversations. The key is to have open dialogue between team members so these ideas can come to light and the right people present in these conversations recognize when a magical idea is perfect for a project.

Practical tools to foster collaboration include informal meeting spaces in the studio and periodically scheduling pin-ups for a wider group of designers to give input and help the team clarify their ideas. Over the past few years I have coordinated a series of these in-house pin-ups, where we have tried to utilize the collective design talent in the office by focusing on an individual project around the end of schematic design. To make these sessions productive, I have learned the following lessons: first, the team presenting the project should not lecture; presentations should be kept short, and the majority of the time should be dedicated to interactive discussions. Second, keep the review group small; if more than ten people are in the room, side discussions will always form and the group focus gets lost. Finally, a wide variety of viewpoints makes for the most interesting discussions: young and old, disciplines ranging from landscape to graphics, technical architects, and conceptual designers.

ENGINEERS AND CONSULTANTS

When architects collaborate with engineers and the wide variety of consultants, a clear agenda is needed for each meeting or else the conversation can get mired in minutiae. Collaboration between these groups does not depend on each party understanding every intricacy of the design; instead, it depends on distilling down the important areas where the disciplines overlap. I have found that the level of experience of the participants in these collaboration sessions is a key factor; experience brings respect for the other's field and the knowledge of how to focus on the pertinent and to have the foresight to know where problems might evolve.

Successful collaboration with consultants is also dependent on timing—early enough so that an integrated solution is feasible, but not so early as to stifle a completely open design process. The structural options for a building may inform the major concept, such as when we designed a perforated, mass-wall mosque in the middle of the desert out of load bearing cast-in-place concrete; or the civil and plumbing engineers may be integral to the story, such as when we designed a 5-story-tall rain-fed waterfall transferring water from a building's roof to a bio-retention area on the site. Essential to this collaboration are leadership, clear direction, and someone making sure that each specialized team member understands how they fit into the design. Only then can the team members channel the vast number of design options into a solution that is both efficient and graceful.

VIEWS FROM A CROSSOVER CAREER: ARCHITECTURE TO CONSTRUCTION

The essay below is rich with perspectives from someone who has been on both sides of the architect/constructor table. Andrew Deschenes practiced architecture for 20 years prior to switching to construction management. He currently manages the Project Services Group at Consigli Construction—a team of BIM experts; mechanical, electrical, and plumbing (MEP) managers; and project schedulers.

WHAT'S IT LIKE TO BE ON A HIGH-PERFORMING, TRULY COLLABORATIVE TEAM?

Picture this scene: the architects and engineers are working on-site, finishing their designs with the input of subcontractors and the construction manager even as concrete is poured and steel is erected; the owner's project manager has created a collaborative environment where the management team meets for regular meetings and dinners to stay connected; decisions have to be coordinated with the entire team in mind and made quickly to meet the aggressive deadline set by the high-tech company that needs the facility to stay ahead of the competition.

Was this an IPD experience in 2012? No—it was 1995 and the client had managed to assemble a team both experienced enough to do the job and young enough to try something different. It was one of those once in a career projects; everyone pulled together, shared information, worked for the good of the project, and left their egos at the door to design and build a $90-million facility in 14 months.

That experience completely changed my opinion of what is possible in the architecture, engineering, and construction (AEC) industry—that historically antagonistic relationships could change and oft-repeated negative statements about architects and builders could be proven wrong. Repeating that experience, however, has been elusive until recently. There has been renewed interest in collaboration and team-based success strategies with new tools such as BIM, and a largely owner-driven desire to improve how we work.

Challenges certainly remain. Real behavior change is not easy, new types of contracts are difficult to adopt, margins are thinner than ever, and our litigious world has made most people uncertain at best about how to deal with any kind of organizational shifts. At the heart of the matter are three basic elements—education, experience, and attitude—that will help to drive change in our industry.

EDUCATION

I didn't take a "Distrust All Contractors 101" class in design school but it only took a year or two after graduation to learn it from my peers. People's experiences seem to be passed along to those entering the workplace: you inherit someone else's thinking in an informal way. Actually I do remember when I was taught to not trust contractors. Early in my architectural career we were wrapping up a design that was going to be hard bid (fixed price or stipulated lump sum). The general contractors (GCs) were going to be aggressive, the client was a new one for us and very important, and we didn't want anything to go wrong. My project manager drilled into us the idea that our drawings and specs needed to be "bullet proof" or else the contractors would use any inconsistencies or omissions against us to hike up the price with change orders. We spent an extra week scouring the drawings and I still remember how nerve-wracking it was to finally send out the set of documents to be printed, wondering what would come back to haunt us. That "traditional" thinking about contractors, true or not, was reinforced over time and with more experience doing hard-bid work.

My formal source of AEC education (in 1980) didn't help to foster a collaborative perspective on my future career. Some discussion was spent on how to interact with other design disciplines but little that I remember was aimed at creating the sense that it takes a team pulling together to design and construct a building—and this was at a blue collar, hands-on design education institution, not an Ivy League bastion of higher architectural thought.

Hopefully design education is changing. Mine was missing a course that taught students from different disciplines what needs to happen *in between* their practices such as handoffs, the lifecycle of information flow, how to communicate, and reper-cussions for keeping knowledge in silos. These team dynamics are in turn influenced by a variety of delivery methods that might be employed depending on the goals or type of project. I can imagine a class focused on teamwork using guest speakers from the real world who would reveal not just how they do their job but *what they need from the rest of the team* for the project to meet or exceed its goals. Let's face it—for any of us to be successful more than once, we need to learn how to work together and bring out the best in each of us as team members. And we need to be seeding the future of our profession with the right ideas now if we want to see them in practice going forward.

EXPERIENCE

After my early design experiences with hard-bid projects, I had a long string of projects for one client who saw the value in working with a small group of design and construction firms that understood their business, had a transparent process for fees, and competitively bid the construction subcontracts. The combination of shared client understanding, open book policy with the client, and the ability to maintain a competitive environment for bidding showed me what a refined process could look like. Efficiencies were gained, a corporate memory was developed amongst the team to reinforce good practices, and together we learned from our mistakes. It's a great project delivery model but is difficult to maintain because owners don't often have a steady stream of projects, key team members get assigned to other projects, and the benefits of shared team experiences get eroded.

A skilled individual can greatly influence the potential of a team to collaborate and perform at a high level, and can compensate for a lack of shared project time. One of my all-time favorite construction superintendents had an architectural education, deep construction experience, and the ability to communicate with almost anyone. He sketched as well as any architect, understood design intent but could also light up a poorly performing subcontractor with the best of them. His experiences across the AEC spectrum made him a high performer, a magnet for the entire project team, and clients trusted him. He led a group of us (our construction team) to a lecture by the famous architect whose building we'd be working on soon; he thought it would be great to understand the architect's underlying theories to figure out why he designed some of the stuff he did—so when issues inevitably came up in the field, maybe he could make some appropriate suggestions. People like this are rare, but are wonderful role models for collaborative behavior.

Recently there has been a trend: BIM coordinators or managers at construction management firms who started their careers in architecture and jumped over the fence to construction. They have an influence on team dynamics because they lived the design process and now have some insight into the issues involved in construction. They help to mediate the discussions, ask for the right information at the right time, and provide a level of shared understanding with the design team. These technicians are going to be valuable players in the business of collaboration in a few years when they assume positions of greater responsibility. A professional degree program in architecture can prepare students for a career in construction as a *primary* career, not necessarily as an *alternate* career.

One of the benefits of having people with these kinds of experiences and past relationships is that the entire team jumps up the trust/learning/collaboration curve quickly. When you team with people with whom you are fundamentally aligned (or have worked with successfully in the past), you don't have to spend time figuring anything out—you can get right to work.

ATTITUDE

Unfortunately, good behavior can't be mandated through a contract. Therefore, a desire to work collaboratively and an appreciation for the value of teamwork are important prerequisites. Below are some personal observations that may facilitate collaborative work.

- It is helpful to establish personal connections because contracts are easy with people you know you can work with.

- Peer-to-peer connections are sometimes overlooked but are usually critical—collaboration has to happen through the entire team, not just at the top.

- Peers at every level need to be trusted to connect with one another and then work the established process. When simple, day-to-day decisions need to go up one side of the ladder and back down again, you're in for a frustrating experience.

- Collaboration usually doesn't just happen; it happens by intention and design.

- The efficiencies gained by good existing relationships might be difficult to quantify but I think it's possible to have competitive bidding *and* collaboration.

- Establish a connected team: make it the expectation and then reinforce it by co-locating the design and construction team, hosting dinners, scheduling frequent project management team meetings, and requiring team responses and team solutions to the inevitable problems.

- The cost of co-location can be zero or close to it; regular team dinners, in the overall scheme of a large project, cost a fraction of a percent of construction and can head off delays and miscommunication worth real time and money.

- Leadership should set expectations from inception; there may be some backsliding behavior that needs to be corrected. Some team members may adjust, some may not be able to at all.

- Strong leadership mandating that anything less than a team response will be rejected sends a clear message that everyone must work together.

MORPHOSIS' PHARE TOWER: LESSONS FOR ADVANCED PRACTICE

Stephen Dent, in the case study below, describes a process of collaborative design on a competition-winning work of architecture from which he extracts important insights. Stephen D. Dent, AIA, is a Professor at the University of New Mexico School of Architecture and Planning and a Partner in Dent & Nordhaus Architects, LLC.

Prologue: A major international design competition for a 1.5-million-square-foot tower located at the edge of Paris was held in the fall of 2006. The building was to be an example of groundbreaking architecture and a model of sustainable development using new technologies. Morphosis' design for "La Tour Phare" (the Phare Tower or Lighthouse Tower) was selected from among the designs submitted by the star-studded field of invited architectural firms. This was, by far, the largest and most complex commission that Morphosis had received up to that time.

The conference room in Santa Monica is crowded. It's a warm day in May 2007, and the Parisian clients and consultants are meeting with the Los Angeles designers and consultants to review progress on the design of the Phare Tower. Morphosis principal Thom Mayne is not here yet, but project manager Tim Christ is running the meeting. The agenda takes participants through a list of concerns and issues that have arisen as the design has evolved since the competition scheme was selected in November 2006. The list is long and detailed, as one would expect for a 68-story, 1.5-million-square-foot office tower. Tough questions and observations come from the experienced client—Unibail is a major European developer. All of the team leaders at Morphosis are in attendance, and answers to the client come from the designer with the responsibility for that specific area of the project.

This recognition of responsibility is a major factor in the commitment of this mostly young design team. They are given complex and demanding tasks on large, spatially adventurous projects almost from their first day in the office. In many cases, if not most, they work on the front end of the design process, where their academic training is of most use. But soon they are working on teams that are addressing difficult technical problems. They learn quickly and are expected to present the results and be questioned on them.

Yesterday's meeting lasted most of the day and covered a multitude of space planning questions, refinements, problems, codes, and details. The discussion today is about mechanical, electrical, and structural issues. A difficult site and a plan that is enclosed by a skin that is curvilinear in both plan and section complicate the building's structure: At this time, it is a composite of the exterior steel "diagrid," a concrete core, and a variety of horizontal support and connection conditions and materials. The preliminary structural evaluation reveals that recent revisions have made the structural concept work but that significant weight savings are still possible. Typically, French high-rises have concrete structural frames; steel frames are seldom used due to higher construction costs. But this site has limited points of ground contact due to rail lines and a highway beneath and the requirement for a large opening at the base for a pedestrian connection. Reducing weight is critical for foundation design and construction. Project manager Christ notes that recent structural revisions have increased the depth of beams to reduce weight for big savings. The architects and structural engineers will continue to explore structural changes to simplify the overall system and save money.

But less weight means more steel, which means higher costs. Discussion on this topic is a mix of concerns for future exploration. (As the design evolves and cost estimates are based on more detailed drawings, the structure goes through a big simplification in the spring of 2008. The diagrid is radically modified to permit the vertical forces to be carried on diagonally braced structural members that are perpendicular on the façade but slope in or out to maintain the form of the building. Numerous details must be modified or created, but design time for modifications is cheap compared to the savings in construction costs. However, in hindsight, one could question the original structural system choice for a building form of this complexity in both plan and section as the diagrid on a non-symmetrical form requires hundreds of different sizes for the structural components.)

The electrical system in large buildings generally has relatively few spatial implications beyond properly located and sized equipment rooms and shafts. But the consequences of the design decision to locate the lobby above the eight-story high pasarelle (pedestrian opening through the building) are intriguing. It makes for an extraordinary arrival sequence, as almost all employees and visitors to the building ride the escalator to the multilevel sky-lobby and then proceed via elevator to their destination. This spatial decision is accepted by all parties as critical to the building's design and is not questioned. One result will be higher than normal electrical energy use for the vertical transportation component. The discussion addresses whether the total number of elevators is correct or if some may be eliminated. In addition, the estimate of electrical use anticipates a continuing future increase in the number of portable electrical devices used by building occupants that will adversely impact "plug loads" in the overall building energy use.

Has the relative inexperience of the design team in this building type led to too many elevators or escalators? Will the estimate of plug loads prove to be correct? Or will advances in circuitry and efficiency minimize this huge electrical load as a problem in the future? Are the clients being conservative or generous in their specification?

Extensive time is now devoted to a discussion of the mechanical system. The current drawings reflect an early decision to use individually controlled air handling units

(AHUs) that maximize user comfort and minimize overall energy use. Additionally, in moderate weather, the AHUs would provide almost free cooling, with outside air circulated by their fans powered by electricity generated by rooftop wind turbines. Given the generally cool climate in Paris, this is a significant saving. However, the clients bring up several points that complicate matters. The under-floor units must be serviced at least once a year and have their filters changed to maintain optimum efficiency, plus they must be inspected by the *pompiers* (fire inspectors) to ensure that their exterior fire dampers work properly. Given the huge scale of the project, it would require several full-time employees just to service the units, and this could eliminate projected savings in operating costs. In addition, the individual AHUs constrain interior space layout and partition placement in order to avoid conflicts with floor access panels and also complicate the traditional separation of owner and tenant responsibility.

Is this an example of the downside of an integrated design team making a decision too soon? Changing systems will require numerous alterations to the drawings by all parties: details, floor-to-floor heights, office layouts, and more.

The discussion turns to alternatives when Morphosis Principal Mayne arrives from New York. He listens briefly to the conversation and is concerned about various issues related to the cooling and ventilation systems. He reminds the assembled team about the design intentions for the building:

> *Architecture is often attacked for being form-dominated while at the same time it is inefficient and is not sustainable. This building is didactic in expressing sustainable design and it's a beautiful object. Performance, cost, and energy are all important. The wind turbines assist in creating ventilation and cooling savings plus they convey the political impact of demonstrated environmental responsibility. There are always plusses and minuses. When I ask Peter [one of the mechanical consultants], "How does this work?" I want to hear we've done something. I'm interested in the intangibles.*

The discussion then turns to resolving the issue at hand. If the individual AHUs are problematic, then what is the next alternative that is highly efficient? The mechanical consultants have also looked at chilled beams, a radiant cooling system that is popular in Europe, though with far fewer American applications. They can't be as well integrated into the wind-powered ventilation system, but they have minimal maintenance costs and, being in the ceiling, they don't conflict with furniture arrangements. The engineers' presentation in Paris two weeks earlier was not well received, and they were pushed to get more data to help make the system decision. Mayne asks, "What is the bottom line?" For example, in the San Francisco Federal Building, the dollar amount for energy savings was almost matched with reduced equipment maintenance. Mayne notes, "I'm flexible about the system, but I want the numbers."

Today, the engineers say they have calculated that there is an increase of about 3 percent in operating costs with the chilled beams, and they are working to improve chiller efficiency and increase the hours they can use free cooling from the ventilation system. Using the chilled beams will also allow the raised floor to be reduced from 10 to 6 inches, which could save significant money on the façade by reducing its overall height by the equivalent of two stories.

The mechanical system decision is emblematic of the complexity of the building design as a whole. The costs for construction and operation are huge, and decisions for this innovative project can't be made on non-existent precedents. Analysis is demanded and it is intertwined with a cascade of design decisions. All building design and construction details (wall surface area, construction section, thermal mass, glazing, shading, ventilation strategies, electric lighting, daylighting, etc.) affect the heating and cooling loads and, consequently, the heating, ventilation, and air conditioning (HVAC) system design. When is the appropriate time to select systems?

Early incorporation of all consultants is a given in integrated practice. When the design and systems are generally conventional, early system selection decisions have relatively minimal impact. When edges are pushed, all parties are challenged by the evolving nature of the design. Significant system changes cause additional consequences, as the team gets further into the refinement of the building. Without the shared use of a building information model (BIM) by all parties, this process would be difficult if not impossible.

The meeting described above is fairly typical of design phase meetings at any office. But there are several exceptions to the norm. The biggest difference is that this meeting is being held in the middle of the schematic design phase, though the level of detail in many aspects is much more akin to discussions that would be held during the design development phase. How did the design team get into this level of detail so quickly? A short answer is by using BIM and Morphosis' version of integrated practice as applied in the design process.

DESIGN PROCESS

ANALYSIS AND DESIGN

As all good design teams know, understanding the real nature of the problem is critical. This is not always direct or easy. At the point of problem identification, all members of the design team, including user groups and consultants, are encouraged to challenge any and all assumptions relative to pragmatics, function, budget—and any previously stated or unstated intentions. All views and opinions seem to be respected. The end result is an expansion, revision, or re-statement of the program or project statement provided by the owner or competition.

Mayne is committed to a team process that is best likened to an advanced and enlightened design studio in architecture school. Consequently, internal design reviews have more in common with a studio discussion than the more typical office review of markups led by a senior partner or project manager, though the end result is similar. Questions are asked of and encouraged from all participants in a way that engenders healthy competitiveness among the design staff while maintaining a support system for junior members. He willingly gives credit in publications to all individual members of the design team on a project.

CLEAR DEFINITION OF CONSTRAINTS AND OPPORTUNITIES

Work in this area is generally focused on program, site, and budget. For the Phare Tower, the specifics of the site and competition guidelines were highly influential in the evolution of the form as it meets the ground, especially in the way it responds to the highway, train lines, required opening (the pasarelle), and minimal possible points of bearing. But as with all complex projects, there are further details to be considered that take more digging, such as a requirement in the development guidelines for providing dining facilities for all employees within the building. On a different project, a detailed evaluation of the climate of San Francisco offered the opportunity to create comfortable conditions in the San Francisco Federal Building in more than 98 percent of the summer hours without refrigerated air conditioning if the proper shading, mass, ventilation, and insulation were coordinated. In this example, Morphosis was willing to take a calculated design risk on this opportunity, which was integral to the entire design and its resulting acclaim.

THE 3-D CENTRIC OFFICE

Conceptual designs are developed almost totally in 3-D by the design team. Plans are drawn and building functions are tested against program requirements. But spatial relations and qualities are analyzed repeatedly in 3-D models and drawings. Plans aren't worked out and the building "extruded" from them; rather, the nature and quality of the spaces are intended to come together in support of the overall composition. The use of BIM software plus the extensive use of 3-D model printers and laser cutters keeps almost all design work in three dimensions. The markups by the design team are the principal exception to the above.

ACCELERATED DESIGN FEEDBACK LOOP

Numerous design variations are developed and modeled in drawings and 3-D printed models. Design revisions and variations are developed in 3-D drawings during the day and converted to models overnight through the use of several 3-D printers and laser cutters. The printers run for up to 12 hours with the new input files to produce a new model that must then be cleaned and in some cases assembled from several pieces or components. This is a painstaking and time-consuming process that is completed overnight. The designers then have a new model that can be evaluated three dimensionally and again revised or rejected. The process allows an almost continuous 24-hour feedback loop. This is a critical component in the design process and facilitates the rapid development of alternative design concepts and the refinement of accepted concepts. It is also critical to the three-dimensional integration of construction and building systems—particularly as they influence the overall design conception. Visual, functional, and cost implications are discussed and debated with each new model. The evaluation process may be limited to a specific task group or with the entire Morphosis design team on the project—and that may include specific consultants for their unique input. Then the process begins anew.

MALLEABILITY OF SUBSYSTEMS

If the design concept is the driving force, then all subsystems must advance this cause. The structure must be an enabling feature, not a hindrance. It must reinforce and give a physical presence to the concept. The HVAC system type and design, for example, must not be an assumed given, but must be developed in concert with the design. In the same way that the architectural design team is committed to challenging assumptions and modifying the details of the design to accomplish the desired end, the structural and mechanical engineers must be willing to posit several possibilities. They must be willing to evaluate innovative systems for their overall performance, including visual, functional, environmental, and economic factors. In the Phare Tower, the structure has undergone a major evolution from the exterior diagrid to the inclined (inward or outward) columns with diagonal bracing, and is now predominately concrete. The mechanical system changed from unitary air handling units to chilled beams to a conventional variable air volume (VAV) system distributed overhead. The rooftop wind generators were originally conceived to directly drive the fresh-air ventilation system but were decoupled from that specific task. Working in an integrated process, the team can innovate and work toward a common goal while continually improving the design and fostering a creative climate that pulls the best work from all. Despite prejudices held by some architects, a creative engineer is not an oxymoron but a fellow professional who also needs the challenge of doing one's best work to create innovative, cutting-edge architecture. The performance intentions for the project must be made clear at the beginning for consultants, and they must have an early and respected voice. BIM software is ideal for this process but hardly foolproof. All major changes to the model must be approved before being implemented; otherwise, the design can be seriously compromised.

SCHEMATICS OVERLAP WITH DESIGN DEVELOPMENT

As is common in many offices using BIM software, Morphosis' schematic design phase is extended and largely subsumes the design development phase. The BIM software allows for creating something that looks real to start with but works iteratively. Conceptual design is locked in early with enough specificity to be "real" yet allows for refinement. The design team then revises and redefines the 3-D building model in the software and adds information on construction and building systems as it becomes available to continually build a more robust model. Because this digital model incorporates detailed construction and systems information when the schematics are complete, there is much less to do in the traditional design development phase. And, just as important, time for construction documents can be reduced because the digital model contains most required information at the completion of design documents. More time is productively spent on design without a penalty in the documentation phase.

At least that is how it can and often does work. However, initial input decisions are critical to the end result if a trouble-free process is expected. This is less of a problem in more conventional design and construction where specific structural and mechanical systems are agreed upon early and accepted by all parties. But the process can be a bit bumpy in cutting-edge design and construction. For example, specific decisions on the Phare Tower's structural system (external steel tube diagrid) and the HVAC system (distributed air handling units) probably got out ahead of their benefits relative to costs, function, and practicality. They were well conceived as initial decisions that furthered the design intentions of the original concept, but later, cost and maintenance information forced their elimination. BIM systems are often said to be answer-driven and can be perceived as the enemy of the traditional design process since they require numerous initial decisions and inputs before the design and construction has had time to evolve. This doesn't have to be the case. The use of BIM forces the design team to posit a solution in a way that can be clearly evaluated. If the proposed system or detail proves to be impractical or not in conformance with design intentions, changes are called for, and the BIM model is modified. The lesson from Morphosis is to keep processes subordinate to design.

PRACTICE MANAGEMENT

LEADERSHIP

Who is in charge? Who approves the changes mentioned above? Who sets the agenda? Even though the team nature of the integrated process is critical to its success, the team needs a leader. When clients hire Morphosis, they are hiring Mayne, the Pritzker Prize- and AIA Gold Medal-winning head of the firm. He sets the standard for the staff and is critical to the success of the office. He may delegate specific responsibilities for design management, project design, and for approving those changes critical to the development of a project, but he is the recognized face of the office. There are no staff members with his depth and range of experience, and he gets the press and notoriety.

Can the office survive and prosper in the future without Mayne and his leadership? It is hard to imagine Morphosis being the same, but given the embedded talent, it could certainly morph into a new, unique, and successful entity.

QUALITY EMPLOYEES

Morphosis employees have sought out this office and compete for the jobs in an applicant pool that stretches around the world. This is one payoff of the recognition that Morphosis has sought and received. Employees must be both design-oriented thinkers and creative problem solvers, according to Mayne. For a number of years, the quality of an applicant's portfolio was the critical determinant in hiring decisions, followed by recommendations. Now, the elevated graphic quality enabled by digital design software and produced by good students throughout the world makes the portfolio more difficult to evaluate as to design thinking and problem solving. The office now takes personal recommendations from known parties as the most critical hiring input. Because of the need to integrate more technical information early in the design process, a solid technical education in support of great design skill is preferred. Generally, Morphosis prefers to hire people with "enough time to experience reality of practice but not enough to be jaded," according to Tim Christ.

One issue with staffing at Morphosis is turnover. It is not a critical issue, but valuable personnel depart from time to time. How do you keep talented employees from starting their own firms or moving to responsible positions in other firms that may not require as many hours and the pressure of participating in numerous design competitions? Losing employees who are in the office for a year or two is a minor problem; losing those with five or more years of experience creates gaps in project management, leadership, and technical knowledge. Work on complex projects in an environment that relishes challenges and innovation—this is perhaps the greatest inducement to stay. (Note: A number of critical members of the Phare Tower design team have since moved on, including several who are now teaching at architecture schools.)

FIRM CULTURE

The predominant topic of conversation in the office is design. Mayne may set the tone and the originating conceptual ideas, but employees are there to contribute to the creation of the best possible design solution, and their actions and commitment to this end are never in doubt. There are reference books and exotic design periodicals in evidence throughout the office. The design staff, seemingly without exception, is aware of and knowledgeable about current trends and developments in architectural design and theory. They discuss design in general, presentation graphics, details, and materials at lunch on the deck, in team meetings, and in one-to-one consultations. Fostering this office zeitgeist is a major factor in the firm's success.

Living your beliefs is important to the practice. Quality design as an all-encompassing mantra has been most recently demonstrated in Morphosis' new office space in Culver City that is proudly described by employees. It is said to be the largest net-zero building in Los Angeles, and is a space that is more refined than the previous office in Santa Monica and probably reflects a more prosperous and sophisticated practice.

COMMUNICATION

Overlaying the historical output of Morphosis is innovative and quality communication. Inventive design graphics and models marked the early years of the office. The work was so good that Mayne sold limited edition prints of some drawings. Success in design competitions demands excellent graphics and clarity of concept presentation. Architectural communication is not just in the realm of graphics and models but requires an ability to verbalize the ideas and content of a proposal. Mayne is effective in this role, giving clients no doubt as to how the project was approached, analyzed, and resolved.

In a practice that now has projects in multiple countries, communication is a critical factor. Maintaining the more mundane day-to-day communication with consultants, clients, contractors, code officials, etc. is essential. Having sophisticated computer skills enables the transfer of information in many forms and formats. The international nature of the staff allows for communication in a variety of languages and, perhaps more important, a sensitivity to local culture and context. The office has embraced such new technologies as video conferencing, but face-to-face meetings are essential and haven't been replaced.

ADAPTABILITY TO CHANGE

Evolutionary change in design intentions and production methods is a key factor in maintaining the firm's reputation. With regard to the move to a 3-D computerized office over a decade ago, Mayne says,

It was a hunch on my part. It was also about understanding survival. I had no clue what to do. None. But my instinct was that this was more of a revolutionary

thing taking place, not an evolutionary thing. This wasn't just a better machine to do what we were already doing manually. It was something that would completely and totally affect the way we think and conceive architecture, also the way we produce it and document it for construction—the way we think about it for construction.

The subsequent applications of BIM software and integrated practice have been fully embraced in support of delivering their best possible product in the most efficient and creative way.

Morphosis has been successful in adapting to a dramatic change in the scale of projects undertaken in the past decade. Initially, as projects grew in size, joint ventures with local architects were the norm to use local expertise and experienced production staff. However, as the Morphosis staff has gained more experience in large, complex projects, they now prefer to do most of their work in-house. This has been facilitated by BIM and driven by the desire to control the entire design process from schematics to the design detailing in construction documents. To adapt to the functional demands of its growing international practice, Morphosis has opened a second permanent office in New York City and a temporary office in Paris. As the Phare Tower project was refined, largely in Paris, over the next four years there was considerable input from the constructor brought in by the developer. They provided cost information and even built several mock-ups to test the shading system and construction components for a typical exterior bay. When the project goes forward, Morphosis must be ready for the French process whereby the contractor will re-do the construction documents and most of the calculations as they will take on most of the responsibility and liability.

The move of Morphosis into the forefront of sustainable design is consistent with the evolving nature of the practice. The success of the San Francisco Federal Building and its incorporation of sophisticated sustainable design features has become the firm's current signature project. It reflects a conscious effort to give new form to the typical high-rise office building in the current context of concerns with global climate change. However, Mayne talks about the design of the Phare Tower as performance-based. He sees this as a more encompassing and healthier approach because it takes design cues from all aspects of the building problem—function, use patterns, context, climate, materials palette, building systems, and budget—and puts it all together into expressive and high-performance buildings.

Pushing the design envelope has risks if the budget is constrained or not clearly defined. The Phare Tower has had several major changes precipitated by budget issues, especially in the areas of structure and building systems. Morphosis' design process has facilitated its implementation without compromising the design concept.

But one could also say that forceful design got the firm into some of the budget problems. In two recent completed office buildings (Caltrans in Los Angeles and the San Francisco Federal Building) Morphosis were able to bring innovation in design into reality while meeting restrictive budgets. They accomplished this with straight-forward and relatively simple plans, massing, and structures that are layered with secondary skins of much greater complexity and visual interest. The Phare Tower, in contrast, is a complex form that is influenced by a difficult site and greater design aspirations. It is, of necessity, an expensive building. Could it have been simpler and avoided significant budget problems? Of course, but it probably wouldn't have been the competition winner. This is a conundrum that this office has to face in the rarefied world of competition architecture. Many competition winners from major firms are not built due to this conflict between distinctive form making and inadequate budgets. Or, are the problems due to inappropriate design solutions that disregard budget constraints? In the complexities of the real world and real projects, there is no easy answer.

CONCLUSION

Morphosis were selected from an international cast of competitors to design the Phare Tower largely because they had a comprehensive proposal that integrated construction, building systems, and sustainable design into an innovative design. The clients and jury perceived their design as the most technically sophisticated of all the competitors. Contributing to this perception were the detailed drawings and models that supported their presentation and showed building construction sections, system integration, and the seamless incorporation of innovative sustainable design concepts. All aspects were critical to the formal evolution of the proposed design and reflect the design processes and philosophy of the office—and give proof to their value.

As an architectural educator and practitioner, I see some important lessons for the academy and for architectural firms seeking to evolve from an advanced practice such as Morphosis:

- The profession-wide movement to BIM requires a great deal of technical infor-mation and knowledge early in the design process. This puts pressure on both the academy and the profession to provide a solid theoretical and practical understanding of materials, construction, and building systems in a depth seldom addressed in schools of architecture. For schools, the intention should be to prepare students for the evolving needs of the profession but not specifically to train for a particular technology or software package.

- Integrating building systems and construction into the design process encourages the integrated studio experience to be expanded and perhaps sequenced with additional layers of technical input each year.

- Students need fluidity in three-dimensional thinking as well as with 3-D modeling software and printers, and schools need the tools to introduce students to them. The demands of the 3-D-centric office are formidable, and while the current generation of digitally aware students is attuned to this approach, they need access to the right tools to realize their potential.

- Team-based design and communication skills are critical to working within integrated or global practice. More team-based design studios in schools would allow individual participants to interact with our related disciplines to develop comprehensive solutions. This approach can provide an experience that more closely resembles how offices produce complex buildings while fostering the communication skills that are required in professional design teams.

- A solid grounding in architectural research methods and inquiry is mandatory preparation for practice today. Advanced professional offices and their consultants are doing more groundbreaking building-related research for high-profile jobs than is being done in the schools. There are clients and projects that demand to be on the cutting edge and provide the resources to get there.

- A thorough understanding of the local community dynamics and politics related to a project is always needed. This is usually learned quickly in practice—or projects will be abandoned, modified, or delayed. This issue is seldom addressed in school, but can be creatively dealt with in community design centers and profes-sional practice courses.

- The pursuit of high-performance design is an inclusive process that should be taught in the academy, including the traditional virtues of function, cost-effec-tiveness, cultural/user responsiveness, and the evolving field of evidence-based design. Sophisticated clients demand the highest performance, and the consci-entious architect should be the leader in this pursuit now defined by integrated practice.

- Teach the design *and* making of buildings. Easily said, not so easily accom-plished. The first step is to realize the difference between the design of objects and the design of buildings.

Epilogue: After the original case study was completed in 2008 the Phare Tower was refined, with major changes to its structural and mechanical systems and design changes to the entry sequence and numerous smaller details in order to further reduce costs. The structure became predominately concrete and the HVAC system abandoned the chilled beams in favor of a conventional overhead ducted system. By the beginning of 2011 the planning and building permits were granted, but legal actions were filed against the project at that time. These lawsuits were primarily concerned with the appropriateness of the location and size of the project, shading impact on development to the north, and the disruption of pedestrian traffic during construction due to the removal of a bridge carrying about 30,000 pedestrians a day. The location of La Tour Phare in La Défense is the nexus of existing high-rise construction in the Paris region. Several other towers of similar size by Jean Nouvel and Foster & Partners are proposed nearby, while the bridge is to be replaced during construction with a temporary one. The court rejected the lawsuits in May 2012, but the judgments have been appealed. As of spring 2013 the Phare Tower is on hold. A combination of the continuing weak market, high cost of this huge project, the legal appeal, and the resignation of the chief executive of Unibail (the developer) led to the current hold on the project.

NOTES

1. Derek Sivers, 2010, www.ted.com/talks/lang/en/derek_sivers_how_to_start_a_movement.html (accessed August 21, 2012).

2. LEED—Leadership in Energy and Environmental Design.

FIGURE CREDITS

Images are by Andrew Pressman unless otherwise noted.

1.1   Notwithstanding this image of the heroic, solitary designer, cooperation is a natural social characteristic in animal and primate realms. (Robert Weber / The New Yorker Collection / www.cartoonbank.com.)

2.1   Process diagram for managed collaboration.

3.1   Henry Fonda plays an architect in the film *12 Angry Men,* the story of a jury deciding the fate of a man on trial for murder. (Photo by United Artists/Courtesy of Getty Images.)

3.2 and 3.3   Examples of quintessential brainstorming sessions. (Images courtesy of IDEO.)

3.4   Crew resource management (CRM), widely embraced by the aviation industry, is relevant to collaboration in architecture. Pictured here is the cockpit crew for the no. 2 A380's first flight. (© Airbus SAS 2013, photo by P. Masclet.)

3.5   James Gaffigan leading the Juilliard Orchestra in Mahler's Symphony no. 4 at Alice Tully Hall on April 20, 2013. If architecture, according to Goethe, is frozen music, then collaboration is an orchestra playing a symphony. (Photo by Hiroyuki Ito/Getty Images.)

4.1 and 4.2   The hand-drawn sketches capture design thinking in action.

INDEX